EPHESUS

ÖCAL ÖZEREN
Museum Researcher

TEXT	:	ÖCAL ÖZEREN Museum Researcher
TRANSLATION	:	SÜMER DERBENT
PHOTOGRAPHS	:	AHMET ESİN, HALUK ÖZÖZLÜ, NACİ KESKİN,
		TAHSİN AYDOĞMUŞ, ZÜBEYİR F. DERELİ
LAYOUT	:	SEMRA AKBULUT
RECONSTRUCTION COLOURING	:	SEMRA AKBULUT
COLOUR SEPERATION	:	ESER REPRÖDÜKSİYON, HANER OFSET, RENK GRAFİK, ŞAN GRAFİK
PUBLISHED AND PRINTED	:	KESKİN COLOR KARTPOSTALCILIK LTD. ŞTİ. MATBAASI
DISTRIBUTED	:	KESKİN COLOR KARTPOSTALCILIK SAN. VE PAZ. A.Ş.

ANKARA CAD. NO.98 34410 SİRKECİ - İSTANBUL
TEL : 0 (212) 514 17 47 - 514 17 48 - 514 17 49   FAX: 512 09 64

ŞUBE : KIŞLA MAH. 54. SK. GÜNAYDIN APT. NO: 6/B 07040 ANTALYA
TEL: 0 (242) 247 15 41 - 247 16 11   FAX: 247 16 11

1995

ISBN 975-7559-03-2

INDEX

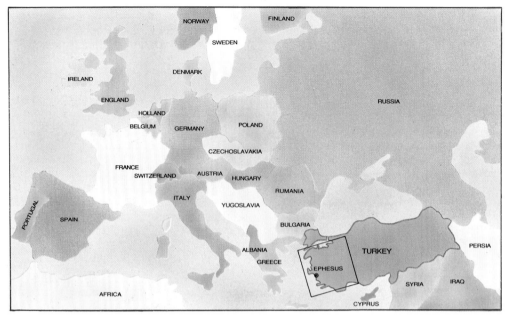

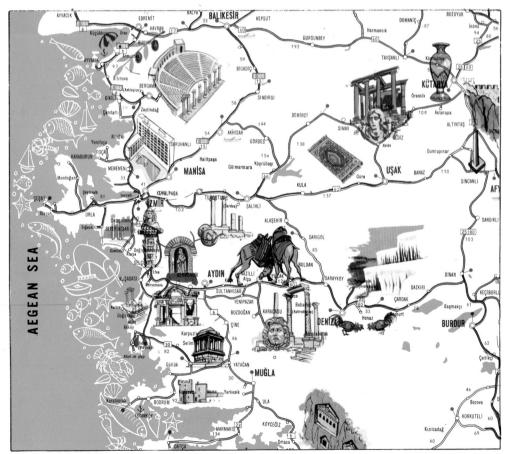

THE NAME "EPHESUS"

In the world in which we live every object and every event which we see or which we cannot see with the eye has a name. It is through these names that they retain a place in our memory. We remember by them, we call by them, and we think by them. When we ask ourselves what these names mean we are faced with a variety of questions which need to be answered. While some of these names are related to legends coming to us from the depths of history, others remind us of events which have given people fear or love, and still others may be the names of important persons. Some of these questions remain unanswered, no work by any grammarian having brought any success, while for others we can very clearly and easily find out what they are and where they derive from. Sometimes conflicts arise. To give some examples, Aphrodisias comes from Aphrodite, the goddess of love and beauty; Athens from Athena, the protective goddess of the city; and Alexandria from the name of the king of Macedonia, founder of the city. As for Ephesus, it has come through history to our day without interruption except for a few instances. Thus, although in 289 BC Lysimachus, a general under Alexander the Great, named the city he built between the mountains of Coressus (Bülbül) and Pion (Panayır) after his wife Arsinoe, it was changed back to Ephesus after the death of Lysimachus. A second change took place in the Christian era concerning the hill which lies today within the boundaries of the present Selçuk and upon which stand the church of St. John and a fortress: it was named "Hagios Theologos" after St. John who was very sacred for Christians. This hill was later called "Altuslocus", Alasaluck" and "Ayasuluk" which is still the present name of the hill.

It should be made clear that in spite of the efforts of a great number of grammarians, it has not been possible to state with certainty where the name "Ephesus" derived from and what it meant. Some researchers say that the city was founded by the Amazons and that the name Ephesus was the name of an Amazon queen. Etymology remains unsatisfactory in this area. Some other researchers maintain that the name derives from "Apasas", the name of the city built by the Hittites in West Anatolia. Still others have written that it derives from the word "Apis" meaning a bee. Indeed, Ephesus was a city which had a bee for its emblem. Also, early Ephesian coins had bees on them. The bee with its qualities of honey - producing and stinging has an important place in mythology. Aristaeus, son of Apollo and the god of hunting and valleys learned apiculture from the nymphs and taught it to human beings. The bee is also related with Artemis of Ephesus. The bee is defined as the symbol of abundance. Maybe Ephesus was the city of a goddess of bees, which is of course also an hypothesis.

Ephesian coin

Ephesian coin

5

FOUNDATION

Towards the end of the 13th century BC the Greek peninsula was invaded by the Dorians coming from the north. The invasion extended as far as the south of the peninsula. Settlements were completely destroyed. The indigenous people living in the region (the Achaeans) could not stand the pressures of the Dorians and they sailed into the Aegean Sea in ships under the command of Androclus, son of King Codrus of Athens and famous for his heroic feats. Sailing by the island of Samos and the Aegean islands, they founded settlements on the coast of West Anatolia. These settlements were cities such as Miletus, Smyrna, Colophon and Ephesus. Thus, they constituted together with the native

the foundation of Ephesus. One of these is that it was founded by women fighters, the Amazons. Cybele, the oldest goddess of Anatolia, as far as we know, appears in Çatalhöyük as a mother goddess beginning from 7000 BC onwards. Artemis of Ephesus is also a mother goddess. The Amazons also had a maternal appearance. The 5th century BC statues of Amazons decorating the Artemis Temple at Ephesus were probably for this reason there. On the other hand, according to the statements of Strabo and Pausanias, Androclus of Athens was the founder of the city. A related story is as follows: "Androclus, son of Codrus of Athens, who wanted to migrate to Anatolia consulted the oracle of Apollo about the city he was going to found there. The oracle told him that

Detail of frieze from the Temple of Hadrian : Androclus and the Boar (2nd century AD)

people of the region the Ionic element. The development and culture resulting from this union was very different from the Dorian culture existing in the Greek peninsula. The new people of Ionia were of an active, bold, noble and lively character. But we will see, in the course of time, this fine attitude turn into intrigues because of political interests.

There are several opinions regarding

a fish and a boar would show him the site where the city was to be built. When Androclus went ashore with his troops, the soldiers lit a fire to cook fish. The fire expanded and a boar ran out from the bushes. Seeing this, Androclus remembered the words of the oracle, jumped on his horse and running after the boar killed it. And on this site he founded the city of Ephesus. (This myth is represented in the frieze of the Temple of Hadrian.)

Ephesian coin

This site is said to be the northern slope of Mount Pion overlooking the harbour.

When Androclus came ashore in the bay of Ephesus, he met the indigenous peoples of Caria and Lydia, and the Lelegs. These people lived around Ayasuluk and the Artemiseum, and on the slopes facing each other of the mountains of Coressus (Bülbül) and Pion (Panayır) and also on the northern slopes of these mountains. Lydians were the resident folk living in the area between the rivers of Hermus (Gediz) and Maeander (Büyükmenderes), who were of Indo-Germanic origin and who spoke Hittite-Luvi. Carians, a mixture of the indigenous people and the Hittites who later came to the area, lived to the south of the Lydians. Lelegs, according to Pausanias, were a people of the myths and probably one of the oldest folks of Anatolia.

Herodotus mentions a Hittite relief on the road from Ephesus to Phocaea. A rock-relief of warriors reminiscent of Hittites can be seen at Karabel on the present day road of Torbalı Kemal Paşa between Ephesus and Sardis. And the fact that a bronze group of Hittite origin dated back to the 13th century BC was found in the area to the east of the Gymnasium of Vedius in Ephesus makes us think that Hittites might have once lived in the region. Could these bronze pieces be considered an indication of the city of Apasas? Ceramics belonging to the 2000s and which can be dated back to the Bronze Age, found in the eastern slopes of the hill of Ayasuluk during excavations and restorations conducted in 1990 by the directorate of the Museum of Ephesus in the Church of St. John and surroundings, takes the Ephesian history known to us up to now about 500 to 800 years further back. Excavation is at present going on in the same area.

After Androclus, his descendants ruled the city in aristocratic monarchy. Because the Temple of Artemis drew large masses here and because there existed a maritime trade extending to inner regions, this small settlement quickly developed and grew. It should be remembered that in those times the Ionians and the Greeks had no important maritime power. The sea was dominated by the Phoenicians. In the 8-6th centuries BC the Greek colonization waves swept the Phoenicians from the Aegean. Up to that time, the Ionians were also in commercial relations with them. After the fall of the Hittite Kingdom in the 1200s BC they had close relationships with Phyrigians of Indo-Germanic origin who had founded kingdoms in Anatolia because Ephesus was a port of landing for goods heading for the Greek peninsula. These economic relations

Hittite King, rock-relief,

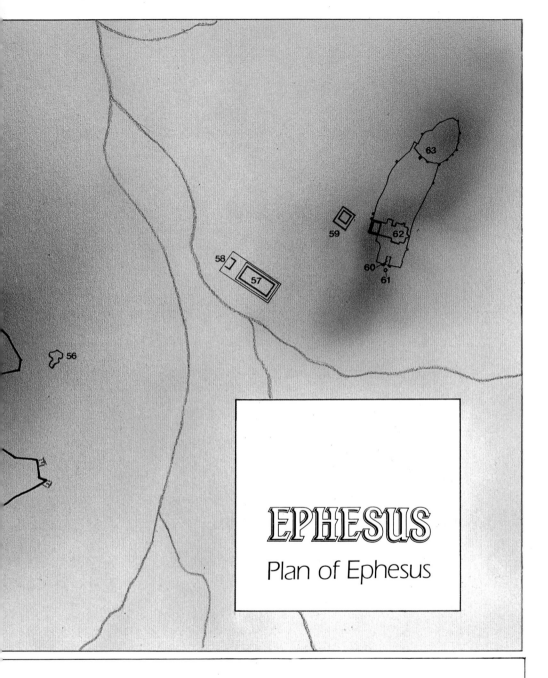

EPHESUS

Plan of Ephesus

played a great role in the development of Ionia and Ephesus. Together
with economic development also a
superior culture was created. As in
those days cities were always open to
attack by external powers, a necessity
was felt to surround them by walls.
Great competition existed among
these cites which were in fact city-
states. In the 9th century BC Ionians
brought the Dorian tribes in western
Anatolia under their domination and
formed a league, and they elected a
basileus to head it. This league had
no political influence, it had only
religious significance. The centre of
the league was Panionion on the
mountain of Mycale (Beşparmak). In
that era, an important happening took
place in Ionia which continued to be
affective to this day. We have no
knowledge about the person who performed it. This important person
created from the Phoenician alphabet
which consisted solely of consonants
a new alphabet comprising vowels
and which could thus be read and
written easily. The Iliad and the
Odyssey repeated verbally up to then
were put into written form by Homer.
The birthplace of this renowned person is said to be Smyrna, however,
cities such as Cyme, Colophon and
Ephesus were cities in which he had
lived or had been a guest of their
basileus.

✦

THE LYDIAN PERIOD

In the first half of the 7th century BC
King Gyges of Lydia assembled his
armies in order to invade his western
neighbours, the Ionian cities, with a
view to opening Sardis, the capital of
Ionia, to the sea. He captured such
cities as Miletus, Magnesia, Smyrna
and Colophon. But in the 675s an
attack by the Cimmerians (a Thracian
and Persian people) stopped this
invasion.

The Cimmerians attacked Anatolia
from the Caucasus, they destroyed

the Phrygian Empire, then, advancing
in waves they captured Lydia and its
capital Sardis, and in 652 BC they
attacked Ephesus. The Ephesians,
although they defended the city heroi-
cally, were not able to resist the
attack of the Cimmerians. A poet by
the name of Callinus stopped the
invaders from pillaging the city of
Ephesus by reciting poetry for them.
The Cimmerians, although giving up
invading the city, destroyed the
Temple of Artemis. And they left certain traces in Ephesus, although little.
The ivory statuette of a ram displayed
in the Artemis Hall of the Museum of
Ephesus is a Cimmerian work from
that period. With the destruction of
the Temple of Artemis, restlessness
began to show up in the city. In the
end the Basitites who ruled the city
were removed. Thus, towards the end
of the 7th century BC Pythagoras
began his tyranny in Ephesus.
Pythagoras had a despotic, tyrannni-
cal and pitiless personality. In his
cruelty he condemned the people
who had taken shelter in the Temple
of Artemis to hunger, thus leading
them to commit suicide. When hunger and epidemic diseases began taking hand of the city Pythagoras consulted his oracles. The oracles told
him to construct tombs for those who
were killed and a temple for the goddess Artemis. Thus, in the beginning
of the 6th century BC the Temple of
Artemis was rebuilt.

In the first half of the 6th century BC
Melas and Pindaros became the
tyrants of Ephesus. Melas was the
son-in-law of King Alyattes of Lydia
and the father of Pindaros who succeeded him. In 560 BC the 35-year
old King Croesus of Lydia, son of
Alyattes, attacked Ephesus. From
what we learn from Herodotus' history
the Ephesians stretched a cable from
the Temple of Artemis to the city
walls. Thus, the city remained within
the sacred area. Croesus attacked at
first, and when there was a breach in

The Artemiseum

the walls of the city, Pindaros, the tyrant of Ephesus, asked for a meeting with King Croesus of Lydia. As Croesus feared the gods he obeyed Artemis and stopped the attack. He asked Pindaros to stop ruling. He did not harm the city and sealed an agreement of friendship. As with other cities which he had conquered, Croesus set a tax on Ephesus, thus including it under Lydian rule. In order to gain the sympathy of Artemis and of the Ephesians, he made presents of golden statues of calves and capitals with reliefs to the Temple of Artemis. He increased the population of the city by enforcing the people living in the region of Mount Pion to live around the Artemiseum. Only the port was left in old Coressus. Following the fall of the tyranny Croesus invited a nobleman by the name of Aristarchus from Athens which was the centre of the colonies to come to Ephesus. He handed the rule of the city over to him. This personality who was provided with great power made reforms for a form of government tending towards democracy. In the new city of which the population augmented because of these reforms, he formed "guilds". The beginning of the end came for the kingdom of Lydia when Croesus, burning with the passion of ruling and the fire of conquering, declared war on his powerful neighbour in the east, the Persians. The result of the war was the occupation of Sardis by the Persians and the end of Croesus. ◆

The Artemiseum, representative drawing (F.Adler)

THE PERSIAN PERIOD

Victories gained by Persians against Lydians brought bad days to the Ephesians. When Cyrus came to Ionia with his commanders Harpagos and Mazares, he occupied the Ionian cities by sacking and pillaging them. Thus, in Ephesus once again tyranny came to rule. The 6th century BC brought only evil to Ionia and Ephesus. The gold wealth of Sardis came into the possession of the Persians. Near the island of Lade in front of the harbour of Miletus nearly the whole of the Ionian maritime fleet was destroyed. The cities were ravaged and destroyed. Revolts against the pressures of the Persians were put to an end. During the revolt,

Ephesus had cautiously remained behind. It had adopted an egoistic policy of waiting to see to which side the victory would move. In the course of history we will often meet with this particularity of Ephesian rulers. This policy of Ephesus did not remain without reward. The city and the Temple of Artemis were not harmed. And Ephesus was looked upon favourably by the Persian king.

In those days Miletus was the most important city of Ionia. A centre of art, literature and science, it was also the centre of a large colonization and at the same time, because of international trade relationships, was a rich city. Whereas Ephesus was quite behind. Did the desire of the Ephesians to remain afloat in times of danger possibly result in augmenting the creative power of its people, thus providing them with a character of capability to go on living? Had the Ephesians not already in the 7th century BC stopped Cimmerian attacks by reciting poetry to them and saved their city from disaster? Indeed, in this period too, developments in art and cultural events followed one another. Around 576 BC the Temple of Hera in Samos, the Temple of Artemis in Ephesus and the Temple of Apollo in Didyma were constructed. The Doric order was developed in the Greek peninsula and the Ionic order in the islands and in West Anatolia.

In the 6th century BC philosophies of nature and the myths began to be explained according to physical principles. Subjects relating to the creation of stars and of the world and the origin of all substances were explained physically. Thus, the first doubts concerning religion began to show up and the idea of a single god was propagated. Myths were denied. Among the first big names such as Thales, Anaximander and Anaximenes of Miletus and Xenophanes of colo-

phon there is also Heracleitus of Ephesus. Heracleitus (540-480 BC) believed that fire had an important property. He therefore claimed fire to be an essential element. (Fire disappeared, air came into existence; the going out of existence of the air created the water.) He believed that in every event and in everything there was a continuous evolution and change. He also thought that everything that affected the senses was both existent and non-existent at that moment (that is to say that it immediately stopped existing and changed into another existence). Heracleitus did not like the way of life of the Ephesians nor did he like the form of government of the city. Therefore, most of the time he tried to avoid crowds and he had the particularity of telling people in the face of their faults in harsh words when necessary. The following anectode relating to this is quite interesting. Heracleitus was one day playing a game of osselets near the Temple of Artemis. When Ephesians gathered around him and watched in astonishment he said to them: "Why are you looking on, you immoral people? Or is doing this not better than to govern the state with you people by gossiping?"

The rulers of the city were acting egotistically and in their own interests, thus causing a lack of organization of union in Ionian cities. This situation had negative effects on military matters and on external politics. This lack of organization and discipline probably resulted from fear of the mighty Persian army. However, in 500 BC a revolt began under the leadership of Aristagoras, the tyrant of Miletus. Carians and Lycians also joined in this revolt. An aid of 25 ships had come from Athens and Eretria. The whole Ionian fleet which had anchored in the vicinity of Ephesus reached the city of Sardis through the valley of Cayster and invaded the city. The revolters burned and destroyed and pillaged the city until nothing was left standing. This was the first time that they had come together in an action against the Persians. However, this revolt did not last very long. The Persians captured Ionia again. In 494 BC the Ionian fleet was defeated and burned by the Persians in the vicinity of the island of Lade in front of Miletus. The people who were the worst off by this war were those of Miletus and of Chios (Sakız). The inhabitants of Chios took refuge on the shores of Mycale (Karine), and walking by night they came to Ephesus. When they arrived in Ephesus it was the time of the feast of Thermophoria which was held in the months of October and November and in which only married women participated. Ephesians, when they saw at night the armed people of Chios, killed them all, thinking them to be brigands come to assault their women.

In 479 BC the Persian commander Mardonius occupied Athens and its surroundings, but he was defeated by the allied forces and killed in Plataea and his armies had to retreat. This event provided for Athens a first step to power. In 478 BC it founded together with its allies the "Attic-Delian Sea League". The sense of responsibility felt by Athens for this league caused it to undertake the leadership of the league. And this provided the basis for the increase of the political and economic power of Athens and for its rise in culture. In 450 BC Pericles came to rule the state and he became the leader of the Attic-Delian League. The tolerance and self-assurance of the early times turned into conceit. Thus, they abused of this role of leadership. They increased the contributions of the other member-cities of the league. This caused the rival city of Sparta to act for its own wishes and interests. The Peloponnesian War

caused the downfall of the superior culture of the Classical Age. The domination of the Persians ended for Ephesus when it joined the Attic-Delian Sea League in 467 BC. But this time the hegemonia of Athens began. Ephesus paid to the League 7,5 talents in 453 BC, 6 in 444 BC and 7,5 in 436 BC. During the Peloponnesian War which lasted between 431 and 404 BC the Ephesians acted accordingly as to who would win the war. At first, Athens was favoured. For 16 years Ephesus took its place by the side of Athens. This situation changed when Governor Tissaphernes of Sparta conquered Ephesus and thus Sparta began weighing heavier in the balance, so that in 415 BC Ephesus left Athens' side and made a pact of friendship with Sparta. The Athenian commander Thrasyllus, in order to regain possession of the city, anchored his heavily armed ships in Coressus (the harbour of Ephesus) and marched with his soldiers towards the city. But they did not want the city to be sacked. The Ephesians took anvantage of this slow advance to complete their military preparations and attacking the Athenians they forced them to retreat. In 407 BC the Spartans came to the harbour of Ephesus with 70 ships, and when they sank 22 Athenian ships the rest of the Athenian fleet fled to Algispotamai. In 405 BC the Athenians concluded a truce with the Spartans and left Ephesus to the Spartans, victorians of the war. In their gratefulness the Ephesians placed statues of Spartans in the Temple of Artemis. In later times, during the wars undertaken by Spartans against the Persians, Ephesus began serving as an important war base. In the spring of 396 BC King Agesilaus of Sparta came to Ephesus. He made his war preparations here. During that time Ephesus was overrun by soldiers. A military government took the place of the oligarchy. The city became like a garrison. Everywhere

Artemis of Ephesus (2nd century AD)

soldiers disturbed people. They frequently pillaged the valley of Cayster. Because of these the citizens had become pessimistic.

And economically too the city weakened considerably. Just at about this time the Athenians destroyed the Spartan fleet in the vicinity of the island of Cnidus. Ephesus immediately became hostile towards Sparta. What else could be expected, any way? In 391 BC the city became friends again with Sparta. Ephesus was given to the Persians following an agreement made in 386 BC between Admiral Antalcidas of Sparta and King Artaxerxes II of Persia. Thus, this was the third sovereignty of Persians over Ephesus. Moreover, during this period a still more unlucky event for Ephesians happened. The most sacred temple of Artemis in Ephesus was burned in 359 BC by a psychopath who wanted to go down in history. He was caught after the fire and confessed while being beaten that his motive had been to make his name immortal. Naturally, the penalty for such deeds was death without further interrogation. Thus, in the end he had reached his aim. This situation was an abyss for Ephesians, both religiously and economically. The temple had burned down, cult statues, offerings and the treasures of the temple were destroyed. The rebuilding of the temple was begun, but because of lack of finance the work advanced slowly. Rumour went around in the city that the Persians had usurped the temple money. The women of Ephesus donated their personal belongings and jewellery to the temple for it to be finished without further delay. Another important event had taken place the night the temple burned. This was the birth of Alexander the Great, King of Macedonia. Hegesias of Magnesia also indicates that it was because the goddess Artemis had left the temple to be midwife for the mother of Alexander that she had not been able to stop the fire.

Ionians who were hostile to Persians sent ambassadors to King Philip II of Macedonia with the request to remove Persian domination from Ionian cities. Philip II sent Parmenio, one of his best commanders, to Ionia. And in the end Persian domination was put to an end in Ephesus. But this did not last long, and Ephesus came under Persian rule again.

◆

THE PERIOD OF ALEXANDER AND LYSIMACHUS

With Alexander a better era began for Ephesus. In 334 BC Alexander the Great set foot in Asia with his soldiers at Hellespontus (the Dardanelles). The Macedonian and Persian armies met at Granicus (Biga Çayı). The invincible Persian cavalry was defeated by Alexander's forces. Alexander, the winner of this battle, occupied Sardis and came to Ephesus after a journey of four days. He captured the city without any bloodshed, as the Greek mercenaries who heard that the Persians had been defeated took possession of the two Persian men-of-war anchored in the harbour of Ephesus and fled the city. It was thus that Alexander entered Ephesus in 334 BC with no casualties and no resistance. Alexander's first action was to bring back to the city those who had been sent away because of him. He put an end to the oligarchy, and brought in the democratic system. He said that he wanted to meet all expenditures for the construction of the Temple of Artemis which had burned down on the night when he was born. But according to the words of an Ephesian whose name we do not know who said that "it would not be becoming for one god to aid another god" made Alexander give up this wish of his. He expanded the area of refuge of the temple. Perhaps Alexander wanted to make himself immortal through this temple, as he had wanted that an inscription in his name be put in it. He ordered that the taxes which were paid previously to the Persians be paid from now on to the priests of Artemis. Alexander the Great, as the beginner of a new era, destroyed the military power of Sparta. With the democratic order which he brought, religion began to lose its domination over the people. Some people even became atheists. Philosophers like Plato and Aristotle attempted to find out the truth about the facts of life. Alexander the Great died at the age of 33 in Babylon in 323 Bc. A kingdom was broken up. His successors fought each other pitilessly in order to divide his heritage among themselves. Ephesus was playing politics once again in order to take its place near the most powerful. This opportunistic attitude was probably a result of the desire to keep standing and to continue to exist. It also led to a lack of self-government.

The kingdom of Alexander was divided into several parts. Seleucus began to rule in Syria, Ptolemy in Egypt, Antigonus in Macedonia and Greece, and Lysimachus in Thrace. Lysimachus was an important commander of Alexander. Ephesus was captured by Antigonus in 319 BC. In 303 Lysimachus went into action against Antigonus. Lysimachus sent his commander Prepelas to Ionia. Ephesus was besieged and occupied. All the ships in the harbour were burned. Antigonus called his son Demetrius to Anatolia for help. And Ephesus was recaptured by him. After a short while Lysimachus joined his army with that of Seleucus Nicator. These fought against the armies of Antigonus at Ipsus in Phrygia in 301 BC. Antigonus was defeated and killed. His son Demetrius fled with the defeated army into the sheltering boundaries of the Temple of Artemis of Ephesus. In 299 BC Lysimachus captured western Anatolia completely. He married Arsinoe, the daughter of his old friend King Ptolemy of Egypt. He reconstructed the city between the mountains of Coressus and Pion. And he named

The Belevi Monument, reconstruction

the city Arsinoe, after his wife. He forced the people living around the Artemiseum to migrate to populate this new city, as the harbour had become marshy with the alluvium carried by the Cayster River. The sea had receded. The newly constructed city was close to the sea. In spite of this, the people did not want to move there. This must have been because of the effect of propaganda from the feelings of the conservatives about new things and the religious people about not leaving the vicinity of the Temple of Artemis. At a conference which took place in the Museum of Ephesus in September 1990 the Head of the Austrian Institute of Archaeology Hofrat Prof. Dr. Gerhard Langmann, basing his speech on information obtained from his excavations in the Agora of Ephesus which are still going on at present, mentioned the following interesting points. In his excavations Prof. Dr. Langmann had found ceramics dating from before Lysimachus (proto geometric). In adddition, he indicated that the site of this new city was a cemetery. Therefore we can say that the people insisted in not going to the new city out of respect for the dead. That those who were forced to go built a wall between the settlement area and the cemetery is also a present topic of discussion.

Then , one day, Lysimachus was very lucky. That day the city had had a lot of rain. Lysiamchus had the sewers of the city stopped up. When the city was inundated, the people were forced to go to the newly constructed city between the mountains of Coressus and Pion. The new city was surrounded by walls. Many people from cities in the region, such as Colophon and Lebedus, were also forced to migrate into this city. As a result, the population of the city increased. New constructions were erected. A modern port was built. The slopes began to be covered with houses. Public buildings were con-

structed. The Ephesians were not happy with these goings on. Many of them wanted Seleucus Nicator. In 281 BC Lysimachus and King Seleucus fought a battle in the valley of Corupedium to the east of Magnesia. Lysimachus was killed in the battle. Those Ephesians who were partisans of Seleucus revolted in the city. And Seleucus occupied the city easily. Lysimachus' wife Arsinoe fled the city and saved herself with difficulty. Arsinoe was renamed Ephesus. In 278 BC Anatolia was invaded by warrior Galatians coming from Thrace. Galatians extended as far as the valley of Hermus. Ionia was saved from Galatian invasion when in 275 BC Antiochus I defeated them. Antiochus won great esteem in Ionia and was given the title of Soter (saviour). In later years, his son Antiochus II who succeeded him in 262 BC came into conflict with King Ptolemy of Egypt, and in order to keep the Ionian cities against him, he declared democratic autonomy in Ionia. In 247 BC Antiochus II was poisoned by his wife Leodike in Ephesus. (According

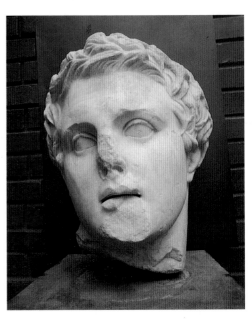

Head of Lysimachus (late 3rd century BC)

to an hypothesis,the Belevi monumental Tomb, standing to the northeast of Ephesus at the fifteenth kilometre of the present Selçuk-Tire highway, belongs to him.) Antiochus II's son Seleucus II succeeded him in 247 BC. He spent his reign fighting Egypt. Although cities like Miletus, Ephesus and Pergamum promised help, when Seleucus II crossed the Taurus Mountains and marched towards Syria, King Ptolemy III of Egypt came with his fleet to the Ionian coast and captured it. Later in

Head of a commander (2nd century AD)

time, Seleucus II and his brother Antiochus came into bad terms with each other which caused a fight between them. It was Antiochus who won the battle. In Ephesus Antiochus III was free of anxiety towards the Romans as he believed that in a probable war Romans would not be able to enter Anatolia. The Romans sent ambassadors to Ephesus. Among these was also the renowned soldier Cornelius Scipio Africanus. The negotiations were not successful. War started. When in the end Antiochus III was defeated by the Romans in

Magnesia ad Sipylum, Ephesus was taken over by them.

The Romans made Antiochus III sign a very severe peace treaty. The Roman soldiers spent the winter in Ephesus. The city became overrun by soldiers. Disturbances and uneasiness began to take place in the city. In 133 BC the Romans left by agreement the rule of Ephesus to the Kingdom of Pergamum. The last king of Pergamum, Attalus III, who was by character a lover of science and research and who appreciated a calm and quiet life died the same year (133 BC). And he put into effect an event unprecedented in history up to that date. He bequeathed the Kingdom of Pergamum to Rome. Thus Ephesus was also attached to Rome.

◆

THE ROMAN PERIOD

The heritage of the Kingdom of Pergamum was in the end not without difficulties. Aristonicus revolted against the Romans for the inheritance of Attalus, son of Eumenes II born from an Ephesian prostitute. And he fought them. For three years Rome tried to put an end to this revolt. And in the end it did. As a result, Aristonicus was kept a prisoner in Ephesus until his death. Ephesians had in this war, as in previous periods, taken sides with the powerful Romans. Naturally, this was not left without reward. And as a result, poverty and debts ended. Manius Aguilius came from Rome with ten high-grade officers as consul in Ephesus. Aguilius strengthened the relations between Ephesus and Rome. He designated Ephesus as the beginning of the King's road. A great number of tradesmen began rushing into Ephesus by land and sea. Welfare had gone up but the Roman taxmen (Publicane) were making

A general view of Ephesus

unjust profit from the city. And they had become quite rich. In 104 BC the Ephesians asked Rome for help to stop this arbitrary behaviour. The task of the agent was undertaken by Artemidorus, the great geographer and orator of the period. Whereupon the Roman senate took sides against the tax collectors who had to take refuge in the shelter area of the Temple of Artemis. And in their gratitude the Ephesians erected a statue to honour Artemidorus. Events of this kind decreased the loyalty of Ephesus towards Rome and turned it into hatred. King Mithradates of Pontus who had been nourished on the idea of a great Asian kingdom took profit of this attitude in 88 BC.

The Ephesians immediately opened their doors to him. When Mithradates felt himself securely in place in Ephesus, he gave orders for absolute death penalty for those who spoke Latin in Ephesus. All the Ephesians who had a grudge against the Romans immediately obeyed this order. First of all, they destroyed the Roman statues of honour in the city and they

attacked the Romans. As Mithradates was of a severe character he acted quite harshly in the city and in the end he appointed a military governor to Ephesus. This situation did not last long. Three years later the Roman consul and army commander Sulla started action to revenge the Romans and captured back the places occupied by Mithradates. In his anger and wish of revenge he fined Ephesus to 20 000 talents. He killed all the Pontic soldiers in the city. Sulla returned to Rome in 84 BC and became dictator there. With the departure of Sulla, the pirates in the Aegean had begun to give fright to the city. Because of fear Ephesus adopted a neutral attitude towards Rome. Maybe it was more reasonable to be as before with the powerful. With this reasoning a beautiful monument was built in Curetes Street to honour C.Memmius, Dictator Sulla's nephew. After Rome annihilated the pirates in the Mediterranean and the Aegean, industry, agriculture and trade began to flourish in Ephesus. In 51 BC the orator and artist Cicero

Columns of the Mercantile Agora (1st century AD)

came to Ephesus as the Proconsul of Rome and gave a conference. After Cicero, Julius Caesar gathered the Asian governors together in Ephesus and he also gave a conference. After which event he invaded Gallia (Gaul) and became a proconsul. In 44 BC Julius Caesar was stabbed in Rome. His two murderers, Brutus and Cassius, took refuge in Ephesus. In 39 BC Antonius (Mark Antony) came to Ephesus in order to finance his military expenditures. The Ephesians who knew his interest in the festivities of Dionysus organized a welcoming ceremony in which they dressed the women as Maenads and the men as Satyrs. Queen Cleopatra of Egypt had also come with Antonius. Thus, the Egyptian religion, the cult of Isis and Serapis, came to Ephesus. In 33 BC in which year his relations with Octavius were getting bad, Antonius came to Ephesus again with Cleopatra. Together with the 200 ships given by Cleopatra the number of ships in his fleet rose to 800. He collected soldiers and completed his preparations. He fled to Egypt when defeated in the sea battle in the outwaters of Athens which he fought against Octavius, once his army mate and brother-in-law and now his worst enemy. When in the following year

Octavius came to Egypt and besieged Alexandria, Antonius and Cleopatra fell into despair and committed suicide (31 BC).

In 27 BC at the age of 33 Octavius was given the title of Augustus by the Roman Senate. And he was declared emperor. Under him internal disorders were calmed. During this period Ephesus began to gain in importance. Also a period of peace which was to last for about a hundred years began. In this period matters of state were rearranged. Persons who had been consuls in Asia were sent as governors. The population of Ephesus had risen to about 200 000 as the capital of the Roman province of Asia. The great historian of the period, Aristeides, defined Ephesus as "Asia's greatest centre of trade and banking". During this time the city was decorated with valuable works of art. After Augustus, Tiberius (14-37 AD) came to power. In his period, in 17 AD there was a violent earthquake in Ephesus. And although this event destroyed the city on a big scale, it regained its beauty through widespread reparations. The importance of Ephesus increased daily. The city became rich. The Ist and 2nd centuries AD were the brightest period of Ephesus. Many of the structures we

The Church of St. John

see in Ephesus today belong to this period, structures such as, the theatre, gymnasium, library and stadium. The renowned orator Aristeides defined Ephesus as "the general bank of Asia and the place of refuge for those in need of credit". In this period, the area within the walls built by Lysimachus was completely filled up with buildings. The earthquakes of 41 and 54 AD also harmed the city considerably. In 60 AD Proconsul Marcus Aefulanus saved the harbour from becoming marshland. Very important persons also became governor to Ephesus.

Emperor Hadrian came in 123 AD to Ephesus. He visited the Aegean islands and went to Rhodes on a yacht provided by the Ephesians. In the spring of 129 AD Hadrian came for a second time to Ephesus, this time by sea from Athens. He stayed a while there. He saved the harbour of the city which was filling up with the alluvium carried by the Carster River. He opened a new bed for the river. In 138 AD, Emperor Antoninus Pius who had previously been governor in Ephesus succeeded Hadrian. He declared Ephesus "the very first and the biggest metropolis of Anatolia". The Vedius Gymnasium in Ephesus was built during the reign of this emperor and it was dedicated to him.

When, in 268 AD, the Temple of Artemis of Ephesus was, because of the riches of the previous period of peace, in its most magnificent period, it was burned down, destroyed and sacked by the Goths arriving from the north. In this period, Christianity began to address large audiences in Ephesus. And later on, when stronger, the city became after Jerusalem and Antioch the third important centre of Christianity. The ideas of St. Paul who had come to Ephesus in 54 AD had reached their purpose. The third general council of the church organized by Emperor Theodosius was held in 431 AD in the church of the Virgin Mary in Ephesus. In 449 AD, this council was held a second time in the church of the Virgin Mary of Ephesus through the great efforts of the followers of the Archbishop of Alexandria, St. Cyril. The doctrine called "Monophysitism" had been accepted by force at this meeting. This doctrine is defined in history as "the brigandage of Ephesus". It was the identification of the Virgin Mary as the mother of God Jesus.

Participants of both meetings spoke of the sad state of lodgings in Ephesus and of the air pollution in the city. In this period, the harbour and its surroundings were filling up with alluvium and becoming marshy. The mosquitoes generated by the marshland were causing epidemic diseases like malaria. Because of these reasons, the harbour was gradually losing its importance, and unhealthy living conditions were causing the city to diminish day by day. The city had started to move slowly to the hill of Ayasuluk on which stood the tomb of St. John.

The earthquakes of 358-365 and 368 AD had also caused considerable damage to the city. Arab forces on campaigns to attack Istanbul in the 7th century AD on the way back attacked Ephesus among other cities of Ionia, and destroyed and burned down and pillaged everywhere. In the third campaign to Istanbul Caliph Suleiman's commander Mesleme spent the winter of 716-717 AD in Ephesus. In this period, walls were built for protection from the Arabs, walls which ran parallel to the Harbour Street and which left such important buildings as the Celsus Library and the Agora, constituting the centre of the city, outside. The population was decreasing day by day. The harbour was turning into marshland. The malaria epidemic was becoming more intense everyday. Tradesmen were going to other ports. And the people had decided to live on the Ayasuluk Hill. In the 10th century AD the city had completely moved to Ayasuluk Hill.

The Theatre

THE SETTLEMENT ON AYASULUK HILL: THE TURKISH PERIOD

The fact that the city built around the church of St. John was surrounded by walls in the 7th century to protect it against attacks from outside is an indication that the city of Ephesus had completely moved to that hill. Part of the walls restored in our day date from that period. Beginning from the 11th century AD the name of the city also is known as "Hagios Theologos", a sacred name for Christians. In later times, because of faulty pronunciation this name appears as "Alto-luogo" meaning high place in Italian. After the arrival of the Turks it was adapted to Turkish and called Ayasuluk.

When we give a brief look at the Turkish period, we see that in the 11th century Sakabey made attacks on Smyrna and its surroundings and captured these areas but could not have a lasting hold on them. This changing of hands went on for about two hundred years as a Turkish-Byzantine struggle. At the time of the Turks' arrival in the region the city on Ayasuluk Hill was a small settlement. Under the Turks the area began to revive. An efficient mutual trade atmosphere was soon created by the mostly animal products produced by the Turks and the industrial products produced by the people already living there. While these friendly relationships were going on, the Moguls began invading

The Mosque of Isa Bey, east façade (1375 AD)

Anatolia from the east in 1243, and the Byzantines took more care in protecting Thrace and the Balkans. Therefore the Seljuks had to remain peaceful for a long time. The Seljuk-Turkish princes who could thus act at ease away from control founded independent principalities under their own name in the areas they lived in. In 1304 the Ayasuluk and Tire region was conquered by Sasa Bey, the son-in-law of Menteşe Bey; however, in 1308 Aydınoğlu Mehmet Bey, a commander of the Principality of Germiyanoğlu, captured the area and founded in his father's name the Principality of Aydınoğlu. As in previous periods, the region began gaining in importance again in the period of Aydınoğlu Mehmet Bey. Shipyards were founded on the coast and a strong fleet was created against external attacks. Umur Bey who succeeded Mehmet Bey also continued friendly relations with Byzantium. The Albanian revolt undertaken against Byzantium in 1337 was put to an end by the aid of Umur Bey. Also in 1346 Osmanoğlu Orhan Bey married the daughter of the Byzantine ex-vizier Emperor John Cantacuzenus with the consent of Umur Bey. In 1348 Venetians who were busy in maritime trade constructed big warehouses on Cayster and on Ayasuluk for the expedition of goods like silk, cloth and leather to Europe. In 1365 with the coming into rule of Isa Bey the capital was moved to Ayasuluk. There are many buildings dating from that period (see the Isa Bey Mosque, the Isa Bey Baths, the Dome). The city developed in a short time. The harbour became active as in previous times. The people prospered. When Yıldırım Beyazıt, after coming into rule in the Principality of Osmanlı, started to organize the unification of the Turkish principalities in Anatolia, the once friendly relations between the principalities of

The Mosque of Isa Bey, entrance

Aydınoğulları and Osmanlı turned into hostility. This unfriendly relation and the changing of hands went on from 1389 to 1426 at which date Ayasuluk was incorporated into the Ottoman Empire completely and definitely. After this, in spite of the fact that it had a strong fortress, Ayasuluk went into decline as the epidemic diseases caused by marshland increased and the harbour filled up with alluvium. Smyrna began to gain in importance in this period. The 17th century traveller Evliya Çelebi mentions that there were about a hundred houses in the city. Ayasuluk which had declined into a small village began to revive in the beginning of the present century due to roads and railways constructed at that time, but its population was about 1000 in the 1927 population census, and 4025 in 1935. The locality is now called by the name of Selçuk given in 1914.

EXCAVATIONS

The city of Ephesus was from centuries back to this day in a state of ruins spread over a very large area. Among these, the remnants above land of buildings such as the harbour baths and the theatre gave an idea of the splendour of the city.

In 1446 a person named Cyriacus from Chios came to Ephesus and searched for the site of the Temple of Artemis with a view to taking possession of the treasures of the temple, but, for all his efforts he could not find it. This problem was only solved in 1869 by John Turtle Wood. The English engineer John Turtle Wood who was working in the construction of the İzmir-Aydın railway, a result of the big industrial evolution of the last century, became interested in the ruins in Ephesus while at work in the region. Thereupon he began to search for the site of the Temple of Artemis which was one of the seven wonders of the ancient world.

In May 1863 the English Government received authorization from the Turkish authorities and began research work. In 1866 excavations began in the Harbour Baths, the Theatre and the Odeum. All the excavators had in mind the idea of finding the site of the Temple of Artemis. Although many artifacts were found these findings did not satisfy the excavators. Then one day John Turtle Wood who knew Greek and Latin found among others an inscription which was written by a Roman by the name of C. Vibius Salutaris to honour Artemis. In this inscription there was a definition of the sacred road used in ceremonies made in the name of Artemis. After one and a half years of

The Mercantile Agora, the Gate of Mazeus and Mithradates, and the Library of Celsus, view before restoration

research done in the direction of this inscription the surrounding wall of the temple built in 6 BC during the time of the Roman emperor Augustus was found for the first time. And on the last day of 1869 the marble floor of the temple was hit. In 1871 the first columns with relief belonging to the temple were found. While excavations were going on in this way, in 1874 they were stopped because very few pieces of work were found. During this time very many valuable pieces of work were carried to London by warships belonging to the British Naval Forces.

Professional excavations were begun in 1895 scientifically by Austrian archaeologists. In 1893 the Austrian Ministry of Culture and Education commissioned Prof. Otto Benndorf to do a widespread excavation. And the Professor chose Ephesus. Prof. Otto Benndorf began excavations in Ephesus on May 20th, 1895 which were continued until 1913 by the Austrian archaeologist R. Heberdey. Within that period the British Museum also sent a team headed by the archaeologist David George to Ephesus to participate in the excavations. In the excavations carried out in 1904-1905 information relating to the 6th century BC temple was brought to light as well as valuable objects such as personal ornaments and statuettes of bronze, ivory and gold.In 1907 excavations were begun on the Agora, the Marble Street, the Curetes Street and the Church of the Virgin Mary, and in 1908 on the Odeum and the Water Palace. In 1911 research was undertaken on the Stadium. And in 1913 excavations on the Temple of Serapis were begun but then interrupted due to the war. During the war, in 1921-1922, the Greeks did excavation in the Church of St. John, headed by a person by the name of G.A. Sotirius. Eight years after the end of the war, in 1926, Joseph Keil, the director of the İzmir

Excavations

Branch of the Austrian Institute of Archaeology began the work again. He gave weight to excavations on the Seven Sleepers, the Vedius Gymnasium, the Harbour and the baths. Between 1931 and 1935 the architect Max Theues and the archaeologist Camillo Praschniker joined Josepn Keil's team and the excavation of the Belevi Monumental Tomb was undertaken. In the autumn of 1935 the excavations were interrupted a second time. In 1954 F. Milltner began the work again for the Austrian Institute of Archaeology. He conducted the excavations around the Odeum and the Municipal Palace (the Prytaneum) for the most part and in 1956 he found the most important Artemis statues of Ephesus in the Municipal Palace. As well as conducting the excavations in a systematic way with modern equipment, F. Miltner also did the restoration of the Temple of Hadrian in 1957. Following the death of F. Miltner in 1959 F. Eichler, the director of the Austrian Institute of Archaeology, took over the work and continued it until 1968. In the course of this period the State

Agora, the Basilica, the Isis Temple, the Laecanius Bassus Fountain and the Archaic Necropolis which formed a complex were revealed and excavation on the houses on the slopes was begun. In 1965 the architect Anton Bammer joined the team and began work on the Temple of Artemis and he continues to work at it. In 1968 Hermann Vetters was appointed director of the Austrian Institute of Archaeology. The same year he undertook the task of directing the excavation. During the twenty years that he stayed at this job he ensured the continuance of the excavations by means of organization and knowledge of excavation techniques, with particular attention and priority given to the excavation and restoration of the houses on the slopes. A second important event of this period was the beginning of the restoraton of the Celsus Library in 1970. This building which we look at with admiration today in Ephesus was completed in 1978. The Hofrat Prof. Dr. Gerhard Langmann, head of the Austrian Institute of Archaeology has been directing the excavation since 1988.

Apart from these works excavation and restoration have been continued by the Museum of Ephesus without interruption since 1970. The work includes:

• excavation and restoration of the Church of St. John and surroundings,

• restoration of the Church of the Virgin Mary,

• excavation and restoration of the 14th century Turkish baths,

• excavation and restoration of the street considered the beginning of the King's Road which goes northwards from the corner where the Marble Street and the Harbour Street cross,

• restoration of the Hellenistic fountain in front of the Theatre,

• restoration of the walls of the west façade of the Theatre.
In 1990 the municipality of Selçuk paid a great courtesy to this work. With the money set aside from the municipality's budget, excavation and restoration on the Odeum and the Prytaneum were begun.

Restoration of the Mosque of Isa Bey and the Church of St. John

THE SETTLEMENT AND PLAN OF THE CITY

In our day the very first place which the name of "Ephesus" makes us think of is the area covered with ruins situated in the valley between the Mountains of Bülbül (Coressus) and Panayır (Pion). The excavations which have been going on for 125 years have revealed that for 4 thousand years the city was concentrated in localities not far from each other. The little hill to the west of the Vedius Gymnasium is known to be the site selected by Androclus, the founder of the city. Altnough early findings were discovered on this hill none could be dated back to the 10th century which is known as the era in which Androclus lived. In the summer of 1954 a tomb from the Mycenaean period was discovered accidentally during works undertaken for a park in front of the processional door of the Church of St. John. These artifacts which are exhibited today in the hall of the tombs of the Museum of Ephesus were introduced to the world of science as belonging to the 15-14th centuries BC and it was thought that the earliest history of Ephesus began at this period. However, hand made rough ceramics uncovered in the summer of 1990 to the east of Ayasuluk fortress between walls made of sun-dried bricks and layers of burned material have been dated back to the beginning of the 2nd millenium. Thus, the known history of Ephesus has gone back five hundred years earlier. The Mycenaean findings belong only to a tomb. It is not yet known whether there was a settle-

The City Walls seen from the Harbour Baths in the sunset

ment there. However, the existence of settlements belonging to this period on either side of Ephesus along the shore makes one think that the existence of a Mycenaean settlement around the hill on which the tombs stand may be possible. Also, the thesis that Mycenaean settlements concentrated on islands close to the shore or on peninsulas weakly connected to the coast, and the fact that Ayasuluk Hill was a peninsula in the Mycenaean period make it seem probable that there may have been a Mycenaean settlement here.

It is known that Lysimachus, a commander under Alexander, who came to rule in Ephesus in the beginning of the 3rd century BC, forced the Ephesians who lived around the Temple of Artemis to move into the city he had rebuilt between the mountains of Coressus and Pion. Scarcely any remains belonging to this city could be revealed. Accepting that the Temple of Artemis following a very old tradition was erected on top of the hill and that in the present day it remains 8 metres below the surface of the land, we can say that the city surrounding it must lie 15-maybe 20-metres deeper. As this area which lies within the boundaries of the present day district of Selcuk is only about 8 metres above sea level, deep borings are impossible.

Quite probably Emperor Lysimachus had founded the city between the moutains of Coressus and Pion with the purpose of making it the capital of his empire. But his life was spent in wars and the capital never materialised. He had to be content with naming the city after his much beloved wife Arsinoe, but this name was soon dropped also and the name Ephesus which was based on an ancient tradition was adopted again. Before the empire shared by the successors of Alexander came into the hands of Lysimachus, the latter had naturally

seen Alexandria in Egypt, Piraeus in Greece, and Priene and Miletus near Ephesus, and had greatly admired in these cities the straight streets and side streets of which one could see one end from the other. He therefore ordered his achitects to build a city with a grid plan (an hippodamic plan) of which the early examples were seen in Priene and Miletus, and the first implementation was executed by Hippodamus of Miletus. The plan was applied in all its rigidity on the undulating land. Streets and side streets crossing each other at right angles planned beforehand were applied as they were on the ground without paying heed to slopes, valleys or glens. Terraces were made between narrow side streets and thus space for settlement was provided. Religious and social buildings were erected at important crossroads. The construction of the city took more than two hundred years. Magnificent new buildings were added during the reigns of the Emperors Augustus and Hadrian. In 17 AD an earthquake destroyed a considerable part of the buildings. The city was reerected by the orders of Emperor Tiberius. The Emperor's decree for aid and reconstruction was put into the form of an inscription and stood on the most important place of Curetes Street to thank him. A little more than three hundred years later another earthquake (355) destroyed Ephesus. The Ephesians had begun to reconstruct the fallen buildings at a great pace when the earthquake of 358 struck them once again. The restoration of the now also economically weakened city was quite difficult. However, the Ephesians began to reerect some of the fallen buildings. But Ephesus, though unconquered by wars and always proud of its beauty and riches, suffered still another earthquake in 365. At a time when money- and power-based relations with neighbouring cities had lost their warmth as a result of the weakening of the central rule and the great deterioration in the economy, the Ephesians began the restoration of their city for a last time. The material from the magnificent buildings destroyed was used for new constructions. Columns and pavements of the main street were made of various kinds of cheap material which were not harmonious. Religious quarrels, and the decline of trade because of the almost complete silting up of the harbour quickened the fall of the city. In the 6th century the population was too reduced to defend the extensive city walls. Therefore new walls were constructed and their extent was reduced. Even then, it was difficult to protect the city against brigands attacking from land and sea. The Ephesians returned again to Ayasuluk Hill where they had originated in the beginning of the 2nd millenium, and the fortress they built on the hill enabled them to live yet a while longer. In the 13th century the Turks, seeing that there was not even a village in the present day Efes, settled directly in the fortress on the hill of St. John. The traveller Ibni Batu who came to the region at the end of that century records that there were Venetian and Genoese consulates in Ephesus and that it was a bishopric. During the period of the Seljuk Turks Ephesus was called Ayasuluk and came to life again. The city of this period developed on both sides of the hill.

A general view of the Theatre and the Agora

THE MAGNESIA GATE AND THE CITY WALLS

The most important places of defense in a city are certainly its walls and gates. Until the period which we call the Roman Peace (Pax Romana) (the 2nd-3rd centuries AD) the gates and walls of cities were constructed strongly and magnificently in Anatolia. With the ending of the Roman Peace the old tradition was continued again. Three important gates of Ephesus are known: the Harbour Gate, the Coressus Gate and the Magnesia Gate.The Corressus Gate has not yet been found. The Magnesia Gate stands on the east side of the city. It is the starting point of important roads which lead to the city of Magnesia, about 30 kilometres distant from this gate, and then, bending into Caria towards Tralles (Aydın), into Anatolia. It was named Magnesia after the first city. Lying 2-3 metres below the ground, it was excavated and partly uncovered.

According to the remains it was a beautiful example of Hellenistic city gates with a courtyard. The entrance of the gate was protected by two high towers of a rectangular plan. In front was a rather large paved square and behind (in the inner side) a narrow courtyard encircled by high walls. If the gate broke under the attacks of the enemy the attackers would come into this court and they would be annihilated under fire from the high walls. Only a part of the courtyard has been excavated. Although in the Hellenistic period the necropolis (the graveyard) of the city began right after the gate, in the Roman period the gate was only a quarter of the city and the suburbs of Ephesus had moved further away.

The walls began at the two sides of the gate and after encircling Ephesus all around they met at the harbour. A very small portion of the north walls were preserved. On the other hand, the walls on Mount Coressus were extant. These walls were fortified at short intervals by rectangular towers. Some of the towers had small doors for sudden attacks which we call exit doors. It is quite difficult in the present day to visit the walls here as the land is undulated. The walls extend for kilometres towards the west running over the summit of the mountain, and forming a sharp corner after a tower in the west which can be seen from almost everywhere in Ephesus they descend towards the harbour. This tower is erroneously mentioned as St. Paul's Prison. It is written in the Bible that St. Paul was not imprisoned in Ephesus. The tower has two storeys and a great number of rooms, therefore it is quite certain that it was used as barracks.

The Magnesia Gate

THE EAST GYMNASIUM

Standing to the west of the Magnesia Gate, this is the first of the remains seen when entering Ephesus from this direction. On the whole it is made of square cut calcareous stone blocks and bricks. The building with the façade on the main street had a columned propylon (entrance structure) projecting a few metres forward. Shops ranged towards the street on two sides of it served this part of the city. As during excavations a number of statues of women were found in the East Gymnasium, a multi-roomed complex building, it is also called the Girls' Gymnasium colloquially. The Emperor's Hall of the Gymnasium lies at the west end. Its bath has the characteristics of Roman baths. It has many rooms and areas which were classes, dormitories and sports areas for youths who were educated and trained there.

In the 6th century a church was built at the corner of the building near the Magnesia Gate so, that corner was already destroyed by then. The floor of the church which had fallen to the basement level is covered with mosaics. Excavation is going on. Restoration is not yet begun in the church or in the Gymnasium.

The East Gymnasium

THE VARIUS BATHS

The vestiges to the east of the Odeum belong to the building called the Varius Baths. The excavation of all the parts of the baths except the cold room has been done, however no restoration has yet been undertaken. The existence of a mosaic paved sports area in the front indicates that in later periods the Varius Baths were used as a gymnasium. The Baths were set on the same level as the Basilica situated in front of the Odeum. As the land was hilly on this side, the rocks were cut to a depth of 6-7 metres and constituted the wall on one side of the building.

The Varius Baths (2nd century AD)

THE ODEUM

Ephesus was governed by a two assembly system of administration. These were the advisory council and the assembly of citizens. The advisory council (Boule) held its meetings in the Odeum. Therefore the building is also called the Bouleuterion. The assembly of citizens was made up of all the Ephesians. On certain days of the year the assembly of citizens held its meetings in the Grand Theatre. The Odeum had the aspect of a small theatre. Its difference from a theatre was that it was once covered. The seating section of the building of which restoration is at present going on, was reached by stepped side streets covered by vaults on two sides. The holding capacity was about 1500. The benches were of marble, and their legs were in the shape of lions' paws. The stage building was two-storeyed. It opened to the inner part by five doors with the centre one built higher than the others.

Plan showing the Odeum and the surrounding buildings

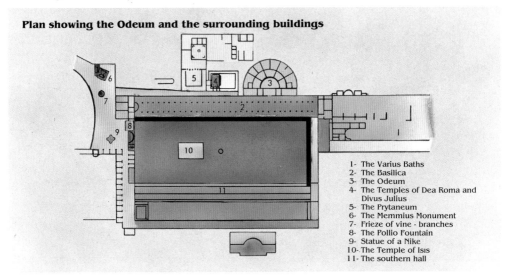

1- The Varius Baths
2- The Basilica
3- The Odeum
4- The Temples of Dea Roma and Divus Julius
5- The Prytaneum
6- The Memmius Monument
7- Frieze of vine - branches
8- The Pollio Fountain
9- Statue of a Nike
10- The Temple of Isis
11- The southern hall

The Odeum (1st century AD)

The Odeum (1st century AD)

THE BASILICA

The Basilica of Ephesus is located between the Odeum and the State Agora. It had three naves and a two-ridged gable roof. The roof was made of wood and no trace of it has been found. Ionic columns with bulls' head reliefs marked the boundaries between the naves. The side facing the Agora had steps from end to end. We can therefore say that this side of the Basilica was completely open.

The statues of Emperor Augustus and his wife Livia which are displayed at present in the Museum of Ephesus were found at the east end of the Basilica in fragments. During the destruction of the building in the 5-6th centuries these statues were also broken up and crosses were marked on their brows. We understand from the statue of Emperor Augustus that the Basilica was constructed in this period. Borings carried out in recent years in the west end of the building reveal that the Basilica was a stoa in the Hellenistic period and that during the reconstruction undertaken in the Agora and its surroundings in the reign of Augustus it was changed into a trade centre and served as an exchange market. Restoration of the Basilica was begun in 1990 by the Museum of Ephesus.

The ruins visible on the level area between the Odeum and the Preytaneum on the north side of the Basilica are the remains of the Temples of Dea Roma and Augustus. Both of these temples were constructed by the order of Emperor Augustus and were completely destroyed in the Byzantine period. These two edifices of white marble of which only the podiums can be seen today were surrounded by porticoes with slender columns.

The Basilica (early 1st century AD)

THE PRYTANEUM

This is the building at the west end of the Odeum and of which a part of the thick columns have been reerected. The Prytaneum was the edifice where the executive council (Prytanes) ruling Ephesus had their meetings, ate their meals, received official guests and honoured them. It was also called the municipality building. The head of the executive committee was called the Prytan and was selected from among the elite families of Ephesus. He had also to be rich because he would pay for most of the expenditures relating to the city from his own budget. The Prytan's essential task was to watch over the cults in the city, to organize the ceremonies and to continue the social life of the city. Furthermore, he had to see that the sacred hearth of Hestia situated in the middle of the building was kept burning perpetually. This hearth was kept alive representing all the hearths in Ephesus.

The square-shaped area made of darker stones in the hall of the building is the place of the sacred hearth. The famous statues of Artemis on display in the Museum of Ephesus were found buried in the Prytaneum. It is understood that at the time of the Iconoclasts the Prytaneum was destroyed but that the destroyers did not dare touch the statues of Artemis.

The Prytaneum, with its façade of six thick columns, had the aspect of a Doric temple. There were double columns in the corners of the main hall in the middle of which stood the sacred hearth. The surrounding buildings served the functions of the Prytaneum. The inscriptions on the columns are the lists of names of the Curetes. The order of priests called the Curetes who were formerly in the temple of Artemis were later given a place in the Prytaneum.

The Prytaneum was built in the 1st century BC. Restoration is going on at present.

Columns of the Prytaneum (1st century BC)

Columns of the Prytaneum (1st century BC)

THE STATE AGORA

There are two agoras in Ephesus: the State Agora and the Trade Agora. The Trade Agora lies to the west of the city near the Celsus Library. The level area looking like a square to the south of the Basilica with not very many remains on it is the famous State Agora of Ephesus. Of the columned portico which once surrounded it on three sides not much remains. In the middle of the square are the remains of a rectangular building which were the foundations of the Temple of Isis. It is known that because of Cleopatra and Antonius the Emperor Augustus did not like Egyptians much. Therefore it is thought that the temple was destroyed during the reign of Augustus. After the destruction of the temple the group of statues Polyphemus which was in the pediment was taken from there and placed on the side of the pool of the Pollio Fountain which was constructed on the west side of the Agora with its face towards the Domitian Square. The ranging of these statues in the pediment of the temple and on the side of the pool of the Pollio Fountain are shown separately today in the Museum of Ephesus. As the statues were dated back to the 1st century BC from a stylistic point of view, it was assumed that the temple was also built at this time. The Agora took its last shape in the period of Augustus. Also the existence of an earlier Agora was learned through borings. A columned road ran along the south side, but in spite of this the north side must have been the main orientation of the Agora. The Prytaneum, the Odeum and the Bouleuterion stood side by side there. The State Agora was used together with the buildings surrounding it as Ephesus' centre of administration.

At its southeast end there was an important cistern of the city, and at its southwest corner stood the Fountain of Laecanius Bassus. This structure of which restoration is not yet begun had a façade with two tiers of columns. With the large pool in front it was of quite a splendid aspect. The statues of Nymphs and Tritons are on display in the Museum of Ephesus.

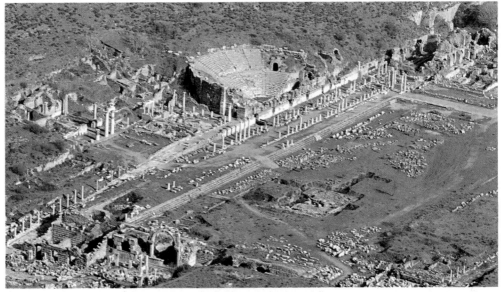

The State Agora seen together with the Basilica and the Odeum

THE DOMITIAN SQUARE

The road on the west side of the Agora leads to Domitian Square. The square is called this because of the temple built on the south side for the Emperor Domitian. At the end of the short road leading to the square there are reliefs of the god Hermes on two bases standing one on the right and the other on the left. In one of these the god has taken a goat and in the other a ram by the horns and is taking them away. Cauldrons on tripods seen in reliefs were used as libation vessels in religious ceremonies. Their short name is tripod.

The excavation of the buildings on the Agora side of the square is completed. No findings could be revealed to indicate the purpose of the construction of the building made of the large squared calcareous stone blocks found here and understood to have been two storeyed. The second storey of this building opened without doubt onto the Agora. From the remains upwards near this two fountains are among the important structures of the square. The fountain of which a high-arched part is restored is called the Pollio Fountain. Following the destruction of the Temple of Isis in the Agora, the statues of the pediment were ranged in a row on the edge of the semicircular pool.

The small vaulted buildings next to the Pollio Fountain were used as shops. These as well as the shops on either side of the temple are an indication that the Domitian Square was an important commercial centre. The existence in Ephesus ruins of shops of a density which would not be seen in other old cities is related to the overseas trade of Ephesus.

The Domitian Square and the fountain

The columned parapet in front of the Temple of Domitian

THE TEMPLE OF DOMITIAN

One of the famous edifices in Ephesus is the temple built for the Emperor Domitian on the terrace to the south of the square. When the Emperor Domitian (81-96 AD) was stabbed to death in the back by a servant of his the temple was dedicated to his father Vespasian and when later Domitian was damned by the people the temple was destroyed and even the name Domitian was erased from the inscriptions. It is famous for being the first temple built for an emperor in Ephesus. In the Roman period the building of temples for emperors was made a matter of honour among similar cities.

The temple stood on the approximately 100 metres long terrace to the south of the square. On the east and west sides of the podium which was surrounded by an eight-stepped crepis were large pediments supported by eight columns each. The long sides between these two had thirteen columns each. This structure made the edifice a prostyle. The altar which was decorated with the reliefs of weapons on display in the Museum of Ephesus stood 10 metres in front of the temple. The Ephesians in order to thank the emperor had his statue made measuring 7 metres together with the base and placed it in the temple. The large head and arm of this statue are on display in the museum. The terrace on which stood the temple was reached from the square by wide steps.

Taking the road running along the east side of the terrace one reaches the cryptoportico of the terrace of the temple which is arranged as a gallery for written documents. Here are displayed some of the inscriptions found in Ephesus together with their translations.

The round base decorated with garlands carried by bulls' heads standing in the middle of the Domitian Square was put there about the middle of the 4th century.

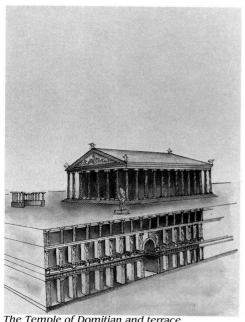

The Temple of Domitian and terrace, representative drawing

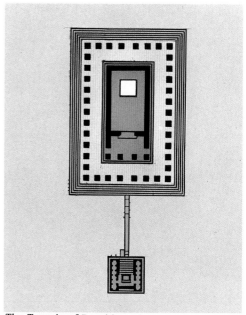

The Temple of Domitian, plan

THE MEMMIUS MONUMENT

This is the partially restored building at the north end of the square. It had four façades and on each of these were semicircular niches linked to each other by arches on which stood blocks with reliefs on them. The high reliefs at the foot of the arches are in the shape of caryatids. Reliefs of soldiers in togas are of Memmius, his father Caicus, and his grandfather the dictator Sulla. On the fragment of the architrave lying today near the building is written "Caius Memmius, the Saviour, son of Caicus, grandson of Cornelius Sulla". The monument was built in the 1st century AD.

To the west of the Memmius monument and adjacent to it is a fountain which was built later. The fountain had four Corinthian columns and a long narrow pool. On four bases in front of the pool stood the statues of

Diocletian, Maximian, Constantius Chlorus, and Galerius (293-305) who were also emperors of Rome. These statues indicate the date of the building. Similar statues stood also in front of the Temple of Hadrian, a favourite building of the Curetes Street below.

Nike (2nd century AD)

The Memmius Monument (1st century BC)

The Pollio Fountain

The Memmius Monument (1st century BC)

THE HERCULES GATE

On the street running downwards from the Memmius Monument stands a monumental gate thought to be built in the 5th century. Only two lintels of the gate have been remounted. The gate was named after two reliefs on these lintels which showed Hercules draped in a lionskin. The gate was constructed with two tiers of columns. The block found in the Domitian Square with Nike in a flying posture holding a wreath in her hand was on the second storey of the gate. The reliefs of Hercules on the lintels are dated back to the 2nd century because of the style. Therefore, with great probability they belong to a structure which was destroyed in the 4th century earthquakes. They must have been brought here later when this gate was built. As this section of the road was narrowed because of the building of the gate and as stairs were built on each side of it, it is understood that the Curetes Street was closed to wheeled traffic in the 5th century.

The Hercules Gate

THE CURETES STREET

The sacred street running round Mount Pion is called the Curetes Street between the Domitian Square and the Celsus Library. The Curetes were the semi-gods famed in mythology by the noise they made. Later an order of priests was created by the same name in Ephesus. These would come out of the Prytaneum in ceremonial costume and in procession (possibly making noise), would reach the square in front of the Celsus Library which marked the end of this street, then passing through the Gate of Hadrian they would go along the skirts of Mount Coressus to Ortygia (8 km), the mythological birthplace of the goddess Artemis. Their mission here was to represent dramatically the birth of Artemis.

The Curetes Street was paved with regular marble blocks. This paving and the columns on the sides of the

The Curetes Street

Relief of Hermes (3rd century AD)

street were repaired lastly in the second half of the 4th century. At a time when Ephesus was weak economically existing pieces were made use of and no new marble cutting material was used. Until the middle of the 4th century the street had on both sides a covered portico with columns, but these porticoes were destroyed at later periods. Behind the porticoes were shops of which only the ones on the library side have been excavated. The statue bases visible in front of the columns were for the statues and busts of the persons who had done useful deeds for the city.

Lower down the street the shops of which the excavation was completed provided entrance to the houses on the terraces by the stairs at their back. As is often the case today also the house was at the back and the

The southern portico of Curetes Street

shop in front. In this section some of the mosaic paving of the floor of the portico has been repaired. The narrow side streets opening onto the main street extend as far as the hills on either side.

The statue on the base found at the beginning of the Curetes Street, as seen from its inscription, belonged to the physician Alexandros.

At the bottom of the street there is a wide sewer. The divisioned circles on the marble pavings were used to play checkers as well as used as sundials.

The Curetes Street

THE FOUNTAIN OF TRAJAN

The partially repaired fountain on the right side of the Curetes Street was dedicated to the Emperor Trajan at the beginning of the 2nd century AD. The dedicatory inscription is today on the cornice near the structure. The fountain had two ornamental pools, in the front and rear,and two tiers of columns. The water flew from the big channel in the middle into the first pool. And on top of the channel there was a big-size statue of the emperor. The base and a part of a foot of the statue are in their original places. When the first pool was filled the water filled the pool in front. Those who needed would use it. During the excavation of the building two statues of Dionysus, one in the nude and one clothed, and one statue of a Satyr in a lying position were found beside the statues belonging to the Trajan family. These statues are on display in the Museum of Ephesus.

The Fountain of Trajan, reconstruction (2nd century AD)

The Fountain of Trajan (97-117 AD)

THE SCHOLASTIKIA BATHS

Located a little below the Fountain of Trajan, th e Scholastikia Baths are one of the important buildings of the Curetes Street. As it was located in the city centre, it must have been a bath where the distinguished families of the city, rather than ordinary people, washed and cleaned themselves and then talked about daily matters. In the Roman period it was in general a tradition to go to the baths in the afternoon. Bathing directly after lunch has caused many a famed Roman to lose his life in the baths. The noble and the rich would usually come to the baths in groups with their ser-vants, be massaged and perfumed, then rest for hours in the section called the tepidarium of the baths discussing meanwhile the important current events. The baths had a great role in the evolution of Roman philosophy.

Together with the ground floor the Scholastikia Baths were built in three storeys. There are practically no remains from the third floor. Therefore it is difficult to say for what purpose and how it was used. The building had two entrances, the first from the Curetes Street and the other from the side street. One entered directly into the cold section called the frigidarium. The statue found together with its base in the east corner belongs to Scholastikia after whom the baths were named and who was the person who had the baths repaired around 400 AD. The building had been built at least 200 years before Scholastikia and was repaired several times. The stepped pool to the west of the cold section was the cold water pool and was used to gain vigour when coming out of the baths as well as when first entering them. Of the hot section called the caldarium the floor paving was ruined but the brick feet supporting the floor and through which the heated air ran were preserved. The greatest particularity of Roman baths is certainly their being heated by hot air circulating below the floor. The hot air coming from the furnace would run through the feet in this section and come to the flues in the walls and after heating the walls would go out.

Baths which developed and reached a climax in the Roman period also survived in the Byzantine era but were totally forgotten in the Middle Ages only to return to monumentality under the Seljuk and Ottoman turks. The Ottoman baths in use in present day Turkey have the same system of heating.

Scholastikia (4 th century AD)

The Scholastikia Baths

THE LATRINA

Entering the first side street on the right hand side after passing the Scholastikia Baths one reaches the famed Latrina of Ephesus. The vaults that once covered the street have fallen down. The spaces on the right belong to the ground floor of the Scholastikia Baths. A little further on one reaches the furnace of the baths. Facing the Latrina, the engraved figure on the foot of the arch belonging to the baths is Artemis of Ephesus. Figures of this kind can be seen quite often on the marbles in Ephesus.

As seen by the marks on its lintel and threshold the Latrina was entered by a double-winged door. In the middle was a pool open to the sky, and at the sides stood the columns supporting the roof covering the sides. The floor was paved with mosaics. The closets were ranged side by side with no partitions between them. Water flew down the narrow channel in front of the closets. The sewage was swept away by water coming from the Scholastikia Baths.

The Latrina (WC)

THE HOUSE OF LOVE

The building following the temple of Hadrian is a house with a peristyle known as the House of Love. The statue of Priapus, called the god Bes, on display in the Museum of Ephesus was found in this house. This statue and the mosaics found on the floor of a room on the west side of the house which showed two women and a man having fun together provided strong argument that this could be a house of love. Of the two-storeyed house only the ground floor was preserved. This floor was paved with mosaics and marble and its walls were covered with frescoes. There was a peristyle in the middle and around it were rooms and halls of various sizes. The entrance of the house was on the Curetes Street. As the house was located on a corner another entrance was provided from the Marble Street. In the Byzantine period the front of the entrance on the Curetes Street was turned into a stoa called Alytarhos. A well still in use today, located on the side next to the Curetes Street, procured water for the house in times of water cut. The house was built in the reign of Emperor Hadrian (117-138 AD) together with the Latrina and the Temple of Hadrian.

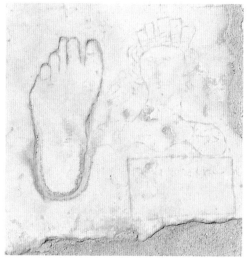

The advertisement on Marble Street indicating the House of Love

The House of Love

THE TEMPLE OF HADRIAN

The most attractive edifice on the Curetes Street is the temple dedicated to the Emperor Hadrian. The Emperor came to Ephesus several times. And at one of these times was built the big temple to the north of the Council Church called the Olypeion and at another the temple of Hadrian. This temple has gained a rightful fame through the rich workmanship on its façade. In front, two columns with Corinthian capitals in the middle and two angular piers also with Corinthian capitals at the sides supported a semicircular pediment of Syrian type. On the keystone of the pediment there is a bust of Tyche, the goddess of the city, wearing a crown on her head. The lintel of the door behind the columns is richly decorated with classical rows of egg and dart moldings. On the front of the upper lintel there is a relief of Medusa in the shape of a young girl among acanthus leaves. In the pronaos the frieze on the upper lintel of the door is a copy; the original is on display in the Museum of Ephesus. The frieze consisted of four parts. On the first three parts from the left were depicted gods and goddesses and the myth of Androclus, the founder of Ephesus, hunting the boar; gods and Amazons; and Amazons and the procession of Dionysus. The subject of the fourth part of the frieze is different. Here are shown side by side from the left Athena, Selena, a man, Apollo, a woman, Androclus, Hercules, Emperor Theodosius, Artemis, the wife and son of Theodosius, and Athena. The inner part of the temple was very simple. As Roman religious buildings were more structures which were not entered their outer parts were constructed particularly osttentatiously. As understood from the inscription on the architrave the edifice was dedicated to the Emperor Hadrian in 138 AD. Statue bases with inscriptions in front of the temple belonged to the bronze statues of Diocletian, Maximian, Constantius Chlorus and Galerius who were emperors at the same time. The statues of the same emperors stood in front of the fountain near the Memmius Monument also.

The Temple of Hadrian, detail (2nd century AD)

The Temple of Hadrian

HOUSES ON THE SLOPES

The buildings located on the slopes to the right of the Curetes Street are known as the houses on the slopes of Ephesus. Two houses were built on each of the areas obtained by terracing the slope. And each of the houses faced a different street. The ruins of houses lying in about the middle section of the Curetes Street which have not been restored were excavated about 30 years ago, and a part of the frescoes and mosaics uncovered were taken to the museum. Later it was decided to display the houses as and where they were, and the decorative elements of the houses such as mosaics and frescoes were put under protection, and restoration on the houses was begun. Of the houses on the same row two of those on the upper terrace are open today to visitors.

The houses on the slopes of Ephesus are quite different from their likes both in their planning and their inner

Houses on the Slopes, peristyle of the 2nd house

arrangement. To say the least no houses planned on slopes were encountered in excavations of houses of the Roman period other than those in Ephesus. In this respect they differ considerably from houses preserved in good condition in Pompeii and other ancient cities. As they stand in the centre of the city they are also known as the houses of the rich or as the palaces on the slopes.

The narrow side streets' opening onto the Curetes Street were terraced for building houses and two houses were erected on each terrace. The side streets were narrow and stepped, and it is believed that some of them were covered with a vaulted roofing. The houses looked quite simple and plain from the outside but they had very decorative interiors.

Of the two houses open to visitors the first can be reached by a stepped road in the middle part of the Curetes Street. The house has a double-winged door. The stairs visible on the right upon entering the house enabled one to go up to the second floor. The second floors are in a completely destroyed state. According to a wide-spread tradition the second floors were reserved for bedrooms. From the entrance door a few steps descended to the ground floor. The fountain standing in the entrance hall where the steps ended was for those who entered the house to clean them-selves. From there one moves on to the peristyle across. In the middle of the peristyle there is a courtyard-like section open to the sky and around this corridors with mosaic floors and behind these, rooms and halls. In the middle of the courtyard-like central section stands a fountain with a sys-tem of running water and its gutter. To the south of this the low vaulted space was where the owner of the house rested on hot summer days. The room on the left is named the theatre room because of the subjects of its frescoes. To the left of the

Houses on the Slopes, fresco depicting "Orestes"

Houses on the Slopes, 2nd house, representative drawing

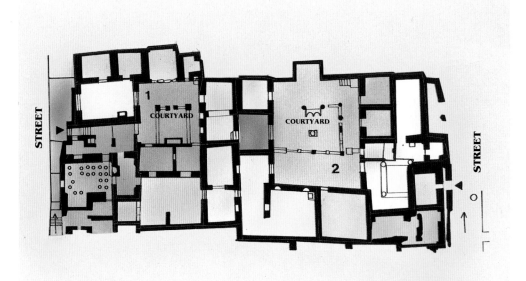

Plan of the Houses on the Slopes (H. Vetters, G. Wiplinger)

entrance opening which is quite large a scene from Euripides' play "Orestes" is depicted. In the Roman period theatre players were all men who used masks as required. Because of this the actors in the fresco were shown wearing masks. On the right there is a scene from the play "Sikyonios" of the comedy writer Menander. And on the upper part of the wide wall on the left is represented the fight between Hercules and Achilles. Achilles who was the greatest river god of Greece wanted to marry Deianeira, the daughter of the King of Calydon. But Deianeira did not want to marry him as she knew that Achilles could take the shape of such beings as a dragon or a bull. Whereupon Hercules intervened and a fight broke out. The girl shown crouching in the fresco is the one the ffight was about.

The north side of the peristyle was changed in the 4th century and the main room of the house which stood there was divided into two little rooms. The traces of fire found in this section also belong to the same period. The upper part of the open section of the peristyle was reconstructed to resemble its ancient models with similar materials.

The rather large space on the right after crossing the opening to the right of the entrance is the bath of the house. Only the infrastructure was preserved of the bath. In the walls are visible flues through which hot air was circulated to heat the house in cold weather in winter. Moving into the left side from here one enters the hall of Muses on this side of the second house which is called House B. The hall was so named because it had frescoes of Muses on its walls. Originally the entrance of the house should have been on the other side,

Peristyle House

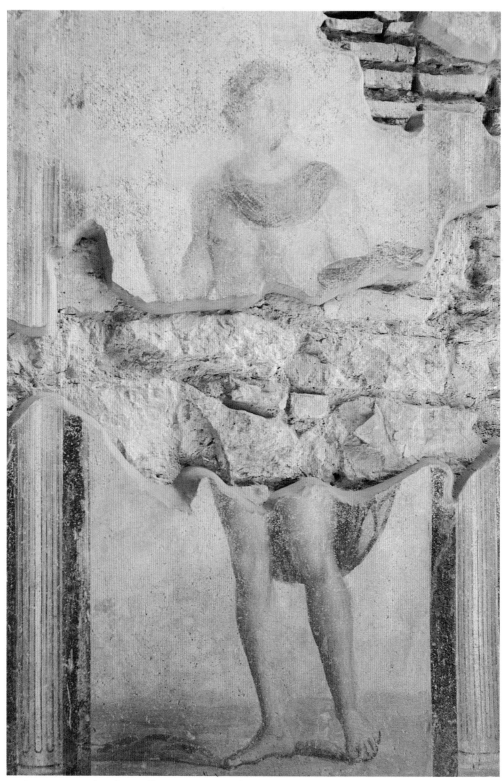

Peristyle House, the Theatre Room

but during restoration it was made this way. From the hall of Muses one enters the peristyle which is exceptionally beautiful. It is similar to that in House A, except that the open section in the middle is larger and more decorative. The Corinthian columns are slender and elegant. The well visible in the middle was used in times of water cut. Glass mosaics were worked onto the vault of the low vaulted section where the owner of the house rested. The mosaics represent Adam and Eve, or, as before Christianity, Dionysus and Ariadne, in a circle in the centre with around them animals such as peacocks, ducks, cocks, etc. which were thought to be present in heaven. The floor of this section is covered with black and white marble of basket-weave design.

Fresco of Eros from the Peristyle House

The last space on the west is the kitchen of the house. The arched hearths at the west wall of the kitchen which is quite narrow are the best preserved among their likes. From here one enters the atrium of the house. As also understood from the construction style the west wall of the atrium belongs to a later period. The original entrance of the house was closed by this wall. House B which covers an area of approximately 900 square metres is among the houses on the slopes a complete house planned with no point missing and including an atrium. The atrium is in the shape of a narrow courtyard. It has columns at the corners and

Detail of the glass mosaics representing Dionysus and Ariadne, from the tablinium of the 2nd Peristyle House

Fresco representing the fight between Hercules and Achilles, from the Theatre Room of the Peristyle House (2nd century AD)

wooden beams between the columns. Appropriate sockets were provided on the columns to facilitate the mounting and dismounting of the wooden beams. At the west corner stands the multi-person WC of the house. At the entrance of the WC there is a lavatory similar to the present day lavatories. The walls here are also completely covered with frescoes. The room next to the WC is the kitchen of the first stage of the house thought to be the 1st century. Coming out of the atrium the room on the left was used as a dining-room. In this room the side facing the peristyle was arranged as a bar. We can assume that the household had their meals here together. The space next to this, looking like a hall, is the most important room of the house called the main room. The owner of the house received his guests here. The floor of this room is covered with plain mosaics at the sides and coloured mosaics in the middle. The sides were monochromic and plain because couches were put on these parts. The red table in the room was discovered in situ. The leg of the table which was quite high was stretched over the couch in a semi-horizontal position and was over-carved to avoid its looking ugly to the diners. The washstands with hot and cold water taps standing on either side of the entrance of this room are an indication that the houses had great facilities. The houses were first built in the 1st century AD and were used to the end of the 6th century.

Fresco depicting "Sikyonios", from the Peristyle House

THE OCTAGON

In front of the houses on the slopes on the Curetes Street of which restoration continues, the polychromic and figured mosaics made in the 4th century AD are quite well-preserved. The portico behind the columns was raised by a few steps as an inclination natural to the street was not possible here. On the left after the mosaics the small building of which only the base remains is known as the Octagon, so named because of its eight sides. The structure is the monumental tomb of the daughter of one of the important persons of the city. The tomb chamber lies lower and is separated from the upper structure by a low vault. The entrance of the chamber was in the shape of a dromos and remained between the houses behind. In the tomb chamber there is a simple sarcophagus made of andesite.

The Octagon was surrounded by richly carved columns and had a roof in the form of a pyramid. The architectural materials of the building which is not yet restored lie near it.

The inscriptions visible on the same side after passing the Octagon are the decree of Emperor Tiberius relating to the restoration of the city and particularly of the city walls after the earthquake of 17 AD. The building following this is a Byzantine fountain constructed on top of a monumental tomb which lay in the same place. The outer side of the walls of the fountain's pool have lozenge-shaped decorations with crosses in the middle, a most significant element of the Byzantine period.

The Octagon

The Octagon, reconstruction
(W. Wilberg-M. Theuer)

THE GATE OF HADRIAN

One other building dedicated to the Emperor Hadrian in Ephesus is the gate standing at the beginning of the road leading to Ortygia at the end of the Curetes Street. In the Roman period when an emperor visited a city it was a tradition to construct a monumental building in his honour. The Gate of Hadrian must have been dedicated to the Emperor upon his coming to Ephesus. The gate faced the Marble Street more than the Curetes Street and provided a passage, besides the Ortygia road, also to another road climbing up towards the houses on the slopes. It had three gateways and three storeys. And it is one of the finest examples of the rich marble carving of the period of Hadrian. Its restoration was begun in 1988 by the Austrian Institute of Archaeology and is not yet completed.

The Gate of Hadrian, representative drawing

THE LIBRARY OF CELSUS

The library which stands in a restored state at the end of the Curetes Street is one of the well-known buildings of Ephesus. Between 105 and 107 Tiberius Julius Celsus Polemaeanus was for one year the governor of the province of Asia in Ephesus. After his death his son Tiberius Julius Aquila built the library as a monumental tomb for his father. Celsus' tomb which is extremely beautiful lies in the narrow tomb chamber below the west wall. The construction was thought to be completed towards the 120s.

The Library of Celsus was destroyed in an earthquake in the 10th century; it was revealed by the excavations of the Austrian Institute of Archaeology in 1904 and was restored between 1970 and 1978.

As the library was built later than the Gate of Mazeus and Mithradates on the left and the structure believed to be an altar on the right, an architecture to cause visual aberration was applied to avoid the library's looking squeezed in between the already existing two buildings. For example, the podium which is reached by a number of steps is arched like a bow with a difference of 15 centimetres between the middle point and the edge. In the same way, the columns in the middle were built higher than the ones at the sides, thus trying to make the building look larger than it was. The statues in the niches of the facade wall were found in the excava-

The Library of Celsus (early 2nd century AD)

The Library of Celsus, statue of Sophia

tions of 1904 and were taken to Vienna; copies of these were put in their original places during restoration. According to the inscriptions on their bases, the statues represent the wisdom (sophia), knowledge (episteme), destiny (ennoia) and virtue (arete) of Celsus.

The columns of the upper storeys are smaller than those of the floor below. They carry triangular and semicircular pediments by turn. The interior of the library is plainer compared to the façade. In the west wall there is a big niche in the form of an apse. In this niche which lies on top of the tomb chamber there was a statue of Celsus. This statue was taken to the Museum of Archaeology of Istanbul. The two rows of niches in the side walls were for bookrolls. In front of the second row there was a wooden balcony. The back of the side walls was kept empty to prevent the books from dampness. Entering by the door on the right one can reach the tomb chamber of Celsus.

A candelabrum with seven branches standing on one of the stairs of the library was probably made by someone from the Jewish community living in Ephesus. To the right, on the

The Library of Celsus, detail

The Library of Celsus, representative drawing of the façade

The Library of Celsus (2nd century AD)

The Mercantile Agora and the Gate of Mazeus-Mithradates

base with inscriptions are listed the regions of the province of Asia of which Celsus was the governor, emphasizing that Celsus was an important personality. In the excavations of 1904 a fountain niche was found adjacent to the podium of the library. Furthermore, the frieze relating to the famous Parthian wars, in the present day on display in Vienna, was discovered arranged on either side of the fountain niche. This frieze is believed to belong to an altar which stood where the ruins are on the left. The sarcophagus directly facing the library was discovered in an excavation carried out here by the museum. According to the inscription on it the sarcophagus belonged to a person called Dionysios.

The front of the library was designed as an auditorium. Thus, on the left were the stairs of the altar, on the west those of the library and on the right those of the stoa of Nero. In the 5th century in which Ephesus had lost its power the city walls were reconstructed and narrowed, and a gate was built in the middle of this auditorium. This gate can be distinguished easily by the difference of construction materials. The sewers coming from the Curetes Street went on, running before the library, to the agora whence it probably reached the sea. The round base in the auditorium on the side bordering the Marble Street was, according to one thesis, the base of a water-clock. The other pieces of the water-clock are on the east portico of the Mercantile Agora. How the watch worked is not known.

THE MERCANTILE AGORA and THE GATE OF MAZEUS AND MITHRADATES

The gate standing near the library provided entrance to the Mercantile Agora of Ephesus and was known by the name of Mazeus - Mithradates according to its inscription. Mazeus and Mithradates who were slaves under the Emperor Augustus were given their liberty and in return they had built this gate to pay for their gratitude to the emperor and his family. This was written on the front walls of the gate, and the letters were in bronze. In the Byzantine period the bronze letters were torn away and only the trace of the writing remained on the marble. The gate had three arched entrances of which the middle one was wider and higher compared

to the others. In the walls of the side entrances there were semicircular niches. The inscription of the niche on the right read that it was forbidden to urinate there. The inscriptions in Greek seen in various parts of the gate related to the trade in the Agora. The gate was built at the beginning of the 1st century AD as seen from the inscription on it.

The Mercantile Agora of Ephesus was entered by the Gate of Mazeus and Mithradates. The Agora had two other gates besides this, one opening onto the west and the other onto the Harbour Street on the north. Of these the west gate was built much more ostentatiously. The sides of the Agora were 111 metres long each. It was first built in the 3rd century BC during the foundation of the city by Lsymachus, and it then underwent quite considerable changes. In excavations carried out in recent years on

The Gate of Mazeus and Mithradates

the west side evidence of early settlements belonging to Archaic Ephesus was found about 6 metres below the ground. According to this it was believed that this could be the quarter of Smyrna mentioned in mythology. The inhabitants of Smyrna migrated from here to the locality known today as Old İzmir and founded the city of Smyrna. Smyrna was also the name of an Amazon.

A row of shops covered by vaults stood on each side of the Agora. Of these the ones on the south are in a much better preserved condition. In front of the shops ran a portico with columns. The sundial with inscriptions dated back to the period of the Emperor Caracalla which is on display in the Museum of Ephesus was found during the excavations of the Agora.

The Library of Celsus and the Gate of Mazeus-Mithradates

The Gate of Mazeus and Mithradates, representative drawing

THE TEMPLE OF SERAPIS

Coming out of the west gate of the Agora, a stepped road on the left led to the temple, This road is not excavated at present. Of the shops to the south of the Agora, the one farthest out was the second road leading to the temple. This is the road used today.

Roman religions did not promise a life after death. Egyption religions inferred reincarnation. Therefore Egyptian religions were also esteemed in Ephesus. A temple of Isis was constructed in the Upper Agora and a temple of Serapis in the vicinity of the Mercantile Agora lower down. The Temple of serapis consisting of a naos and a pronaos was in the form of a typical prostyle. It was built of large blocks of marble of which the weight would be 40-50 tons at first sight. This is a most significant particularity of Egyptian religious buildings. The monolithic columns with Corinthian capitals had a diameter of 1.5 metres. The door of the edifice had two wings and was very wide. As the opening and closing of such big and heavy doors would be difficult, rollers were placed under them. The trace in the form of an arc visible on the stylobate was produced by the movement to and fro of the roller.

It is understood that in front of the

The Temple of Serapis

building there was a courtyard of a length of 160 metres with columns on the sides. The unfinished state of certain construction materials here and in the close vicinity of the edifice show that the Temple of Serapis was not completed.

Trades relations between Egypt and Ephesus had begun before the Hellenistic period and many works of art were brought to Ephesus from Egypt. The foundation of Alexandria togeher with the beginning of the Hellenistic period brought the relations between Egypt and Ephesus to a climax. And although these relations were restricted during the reign of the Emperor Augustus they were revived in the 2nd and 3rd centuries. Depicted in a treaty document on display in the Musuem of Ephesus was a wreath with on one side the greatest goddess of Ephesus, Artemis, and on the other the greatest god of Egypt, Serapis. The god and the godess must have been witnesses to the treaty.

The Temple of Serapis, detail

The Temple of Serapis, representative drawing

THE MARBLE STREET

The part of the Sacred road running between the Library of Celsus and the Grand Theatre is called the Marble Street. The street was paved with large blocks of marble and had her-ring-bone slopes. On the Mount Pion side it had a portico higher than the street level. The other side was turned into a Doric stoa during the reign of the Emperor Nero. Restoration of the stoa is going on at the moment. The wall pattern on the street side of the stoa which lies about 2.5 metres higher than the street level is very beatiful. In the Byzantine period the top part of this wall was pulled down in order to take the irons and leads holding the blocks of stone, and the lower part which could not be destroyed was broken up. Along the middle of the street run the sewers large and deep enough for a small chariot to move in easily. The sewers coming from the direction of Mount Pion run into this. On the stoa side of the street a woman, a left foot and a heart were carved into the marble in a section surrounded by an iron fence. According to some this was the first advertisement in history and was advertising the house of love and showing where it was. Indeed, the house of love was on the left further on. The woman signified that there were women there and the heart that those who wanted could also find love.

The Marble Street

THE THEATRE

The Theatre of Ephesus was first built in the Hellenistic period on the slope of Mount Pion taking anvantage of its height and was later expanded by repairs at various times. When St. Paul came to Ephesus work on the expansion of the Theatre was going on. This is the largest theatre structure in Turkey and has a holding capacity of about 24 000 spectators. The assembly of citizens in which all the Ephesians participated was held once a year in this theatre. When St. Paul came to Ephesus he propagandized on the new religion in this theatre and was opposed by a group of Ephesians. According to St. Paul's Epistle a group entered the Theatre while the Saint was preaching and shouted for hours that Artemis of Ephesus was great. The group was headed by a person called Demetrius the Jeweller. Demetrius made statuettes of the goddess from precious metals and sold these. He thought that with the new religion the statuettes would not sell and called the people to oppose it. In the end a public security officer of the city came and told the mob that the courts were open and that those who had complaints could make their claims there, and thereby subdued them.

In the 3rd and 4th centuries when wild animal fights and gladiator games were in great demand the Theatre was used for this purpose together with the Stadium. Such games were very popular in Ephesus. It is known that

The Theatre

The Hellenistic Fountain

some rich Ephesians owned gladiator schools.

The Theatre, like others, consisted of three main parts: the stage building (skene), the section where the audience sat (cavea), and the circular orchestra in between these two. The orchestra was allocated to the chorus in performances carried out all through antique times. The chorus entered the orchestra in two rows by the side entrances (parados), took its place and spoke simultaneously when their turn came.

The stage building had three storeys including the ground floor. The side of the stage building facing the interior of the Theatre was built very ostentatiously. On this façade there were three-tiered columns, behind these, niches with frontals and inside the niches, statues. It had five doors of which the middle one was larger

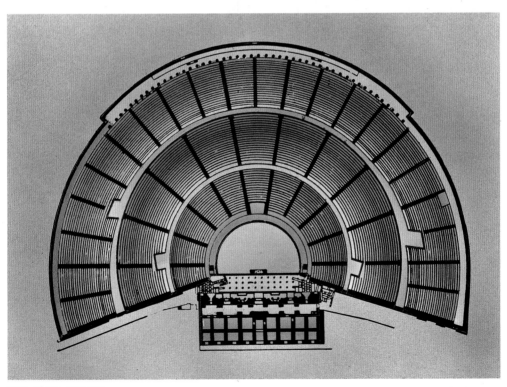
Plan of the Theatre

The Theatre seen from the Harbour Street side

compared to the others. A bust or a statue of the emperor stood in the niche over this middle door. In front of the stage building at a level 2.5 metres above the ground floor was a podium used by the actors. The modern performances of today are wrongly executed on the orchestra floor. The shape of the section where the audience sat exceeded that of a semicircle. It was divided into three parts by two diazomas. The legs of the seats were in the shape of lions' paws. Rubble was used for the bottom and finely worked marble for the top. The ceiling coffer of the box reserved for the emperor lies in the orchestra but its original place is not known. The spectators came to the theatre by the stepped way at the sides of the paradoses. Besides these there was one other door opening onto the road running by the topmost point of the Theatre. Behind the last row of seats a columned portico surrounded the whole structure. This portico, the round shape of the Theatre, the concavity of the bases of the rows of seats were all features that provided the acoustics so necessary in a theatre.

The part of the Theatre facing the Marble Street and the Harbour Street was built very plainly. The little fountain here was built in the Hellenistic period. Water flowed into the pool in front from taps in the form of lions' mouths. The fountain was expanded in the 4th century and two new columns without flutes were put in front of the two slender Ionic columns. The restoration of the structure was completed in 1990. The pool nearby belongs to another fountain built at a later period.

The Theatre

The Theatre, front view of the stage

The Stage Building of the Grand Theatre, representative drawing

THE HARBOUR STREET

The approximately 500 metres long street running between the Theatre and the harbour was called the Harbour Street or the Arcadiana. The street constructed in the 1st century BC was repaired and widened by the Eastern Roman Emperor Arcadius (395-408) and made into a true ceremonial street. It took its ultimate form after the repairs made in this period. It is a meeting point of roads coming from the inner parts of Anatolia and from overseas countries. Many a celebrity came to the harbour from Rome or other cities and walked to the city in ceremony along this road. At both ends of the street on the Theatre and the harbour side there were three-passaged gates in the form of an arch of triumph. Of these gates particularly the one near the Theatre was destroyed down to its foundations.

The street was 11 metres wide and had a portico on either side of which Corinthian columns supported the roof. Behind the portico was a row of shops and stores. The lower parts of the northern side were allocated entirely to sports areas. The thick rubble wall on the south side was the Byzantine city wall of Ephesus. In the Byzantine period the street was left outside the city. In the middle of the street on four tall columns different from the others stood the statues of the four writers of the Bible. Today only one of the columns stands, of the others only the bases have remained.

According to an inscription found during excavations the Harbour Street of Ephesus was illuminated by fifty lamps at night. In the Roman period illuminated cities were quite rare.

The Harbour Street

The Harbour Street

THE HARBOUR

Following the Harbour Street which is approximately 500 metres long one reaches the Harbour of Ephesus which has today turned into a very small lake. In the Hellenistic period and at the beginning of the Roman period the harbour was the best protected mercantile port of the Mediterranean. At the end of the street it opened towards the sea in the form of an ellipse and was connected to it by a narrow channel. This channel was bordered on either side by marble piers. Close to the sea there are the remains of a building once belonging to the Ephesian customs. The width of the harbour can be easily seen from today's outcrop of plants and vegetation. In excavations carried out in the last three years quays, piers and a lot of materials which had been dropped into the sea were discovered. In these excavations were also found very near the quay of the harbour traces of the road beginning at the Curetes Street and reaching Ortygia after passing through the Gate of Hadrian. All through history the harbour of Ephesus was to be continually silted and then each time with great difficulty cleared and made navigable again. At the end of the 4th century it was seen that the clearing process was futile and it was abandoned. Thus, the mercantile harbour to which Ephesus was indebted for its riches was buried into history.

A multi - lined inscription used as an ambo, found during the excavations in the Church of St. John and now on display in the Museum of Ephesus, comprises the Ephesian harbour laws. The inscription also known as the Monument of Ephesus indicated the rates of the customs duties. In the Roman period tax revenue was sold against cash to tax farmers who would collect the taxes as foreseen by the law. The transport of the emperor and the army and personal belongings were not taxed.

The Harbour Street, representative drawing

THE HARBOUR BATHS

A considerable part of the north side of the Harbour Street was allocated to sports grounds. In about the middle of this area was the Verulanus sports ground of which the excavation has not yet been undertaken. It was constructed together with the buildings around it during the reconstruction of that part of the city under the reign of the Emperor Hadrian (117-138). Next to the Verulanus sports ground was the Harbour Gymnasium. The Gymnasium was constructed together with the building called the Harbour Baths. The entrance to it was through an elliptical courtyard in the lower parts of the Harbour Street. The courtyard was paved with coloured mosaics and had porticoes with columns on its sides. Facing the entrance, on either side of the door of the baths were two long and narrow pools of which the façades were decorated with bulls'heads wearing wreaths. The Gymnasium was entered from the right, and the baths from the middle. Neither of these buildings have been restored. Two life-size statues found in the excavations of the Gymnasium,

The Harbour Baths, detail

one a bronze statue of an athlete and the other a marble statue of a child playing with a duck, are on display in the Museum of Vienna. A considerable part of the materials of the baths were used in buildings constructed later. As the baths were repaired during the reign of Constantine II (337-361) they were also called the Constantine Baths. The excavation is not completed.

The Harbour Baths (2nd century AD)

THE THEATRE GYMNASIUM

This was the building located at the beginning of the Harbour Street near the Theatre. The excavation is not completed. It had a palaestra (sports ground) on the street. At the point where the palaestra joined the main building there were rows of seats for those who watched the exercises. The Gymnasium had a great number of rooms which were used as classrooms, dormitories and libraries. The Emperor's Hall in which stood a bust of the emperor was at the northern end. The building faced more towards the Marble Street which continued after the Theatre. From the gymnasium onwards about a 150-metre long section of the street was excavated and part of the columns on either side were erected. A part of this section of the Sacred Road was repaired after the earthquakes of the 4th century and the rest was left as it was. In this section traces left by Roman chariots on the marble paving, reaching in places 10 centimetres in depth, were preserved. The large marble cauldron (omphalos) left at the side of the street in a partly broken state belonged to the unexcavated building nearby. This building, a wall of which was in the form of an apse, is said to be a synagogue. From here a street led west. This not yet excavated street ran along the Church of the Virgin Mary (the Council Church) to reach unknown buildings below.

The Theatre Gymnasium

THE CHURCH OF THE VIRGIN MARY (THE COUNCIL CHURCH)

This edifice is famed for being the first church built for the Virgin Mary. Furthermore, it was the church where the Ecumenical Council of 431 was held. It is therefore among the most important religious buildings of Christianity.

The building can be reached by the narrow road lying across from the ticket box. The excavation is finished and part of the restoration is completed. The Church of the Virgin Mary is one of the buildings in Ephesus whose history is well known. The building had various periods. The first of these was the period when it was used as a museion. That the Virgin Mary, when she came to Ephesus, stayed in a house which stood on the same site before the church was built was recorded in the book of records of the Council. It is not known for what purpose this building termed the Museion was used. According to

some it was the stock exchange building. An inscription found in recent years on the walls of the church mentions that professors who taught in the Museion would not pay customs duties during their travels in the province of Asia. It can be said according to this text that the Museion could have been a medical school. During excavations one came across this first building's walls made of large blocks. Because of this the Museion must have been quite a large building. To the north there is the big Olypeion built to honour the return of Emperor Hadrian to Ephesus from Athens as Zeus Olypios. The marbles of this building were used to produce lime for repairs in later periods. A Corinthian capital uncovered was 1.5 metres high.

The second stage of the building was the church in which the Council of the year 431 met. This building was erected on the exact site of the Museion but was of a smaller plan. The Museion was about 50 metres longer than the church. At the west end of this early church there was a square-shaped atrium paved with ancient marbles. The main entrance of the edifice was by the door on the

The Church of the Virgin Mary

south side of the atrium of which only the foundations are in sight today. Across from the door in a symmetrical position stood the baptistry of the church. This structure had a cupola and was octagonal. The piers supporting the cupola were covered with marble plates with crosses on them. Of the crosses which were of bronze only their traces remain. The font in the middle has stairs on either side. There are also the ruins of a small bath constructed later between the baptistry and the atrium. Tombs lying close together discovered in excavations carried out to the north of the building show that this area was used as a cemetery in the 11th and 12th centuries.

The third stage of the building was a domed church. When the Council Church which had been built in the 420s and used for about a hundred years was destroyed because of some unknown reason a smaller but domed church was built at the beginning of the 6th century (the reign of Justinian) on the exact site where it had stood. With the apse of this new church which stood about 20 metres distant from the apse of the first church the edifice looked like two churches and for this reason it was also called at one period the Double Church of the Virgin Mary. The brick piers supporting the dome of the church were repaired and made more

conspicuous. The door of this church also opened onto the south. When this church too was destroyed also for some unknown reason, in the 10th century a small church with three apses was built in the space between the apses of the former churches and the apse of the first church was used as it was. The little chapel standing towards the street running along the south side of the edifice was also built at the period of this last church.

The Ecumenical Council of Ephesus of the year 431 met in the first church. The topic of debate of that meeting was whether the Virgin Mary was the mother of the god Christ or the human Christ. When the patriarch of Istanbul, during his stay in Antioch, put forward the opinion that the Virgin Mary was the mother of the human Christ big scale discussions arose among the churches which caused uneasiness among the people. Whereupon the Emperor Theodosius ordered a meeting of the Ecumenical Council in Ephesus. The patriarch of Constantinople, Nestorius, the patriarch of Alexandria, the patriarch of Antioch, John, and about two hundred religious participated in the meeting. All the while the meeting went on there was much bloodshed in Ephesus and for three months the city went through frightful days. Following this, in 449 a new meeting of the Council was again held in Ephesus.

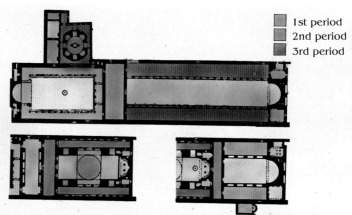

1st period
2nd period
3rd period

Plans of the Church of the Virgin Mary, belonging to three different periods

THE STADIUM

This structure lies at the entrance of the city in the Kuşadası direction. A good example of the stadiums of the period, it is 230 metres long and 30 metres wide. Its entrance is on the west. The entrance with two rows of columns is in the form of an arch of triumph. The stone blocks standing there, decorated with reliefs of figures such as rabbits and vases, were brought from some other place at a later period and were used here for a second time. The rows of seats on the right were made by cutting into the mountain and the ones of the left were set on long vaulted spaces. The Stadium was first built in the Hellenistic period, then was altered in Nero's reign (54-68 AD) for its present shape. In the 3rd and 4th centuries a wall was put up at the east end and an arena was formed where gladiator games, wild animal fights and acrobatic shows took place. With the acceptance of Christianity as the official religion the Stadium was razed to the ground to avenge the cruelty inflicted upon the early Christians and an important part of the material was used in the construction of the Church of St. John and the surrounding walls.

Festival of camel fights in the Stadium

THE VEDIUS GYMNASIUM

According to an inscription discovered in excavations this gymnasium was built by P. Vedius Antonius from the Vedius who were a well-known family of Ephesus and his wife Flavia Papiana. The edifice was dedicated to the goddess Artemis and to the Emperor Antonius Pius (138-161 AD) by its builders. From the many gymnasiums uncovered in Ephesus the most beautiful is without any doubt the Vedius Gymnasium. It has much space and many rooms. In a niche behind the propylaeum which had columns stood a statue of the emperor. To the west of the propylaeum was the group of buildings and to the east the palaestra surrounded by a portico. The very well-preserved

87

The Vedius Gymnasium

latrina lies near the columned gate opening onto the street to the south of the palaestra. The first hall after the propylaeum with its surface of 200 square metres was the imperial and ceremonial hall. The other rooms were used as classrooms and dormitories. The baths were at the west-end. The excavation of the gymnasium is not completed.

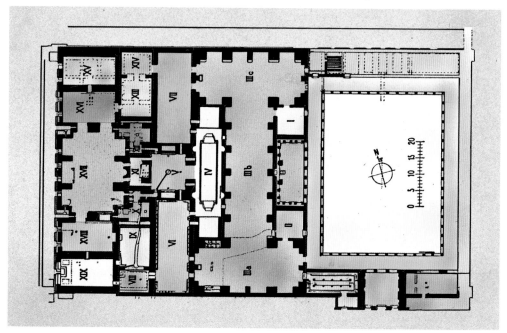

Plan of the Vedius Gymnasium

THE CHURCH OF St. JOHN

This church is located to the south of the fortress in the district of Selcuk. The Church of Ephesus was founded by St. Paul and carried on by St. John. According to St. John's Gospel Christ had entrusted his mother to St. John before being crucified. Seeing their lives in danger in Jerusalem St. John came to Ephesus with the Virgin Mary. Ephesus was one of the most modern and tolerant cities of the time. In those days people of all religions could worship their cult without any difficulty. Therefore their coming to Ephesus was not accidental. In spite of his old age St. John tried to propagate the new religion. When he died he was buried according to his wishes in the church of which we see the remains today and in the 4th century a small basilica was con-

The Church of St. John

The Church of St. John, representative drawing

The Church of St. John

The Fortress on Ayasuluk Hill and the Church of St. John

A general view of Ayasuluk Hill

structed on his tomb. And in the reign of the Emperor Justinian the present church was built. The Church of St. John was of a size and beauty to compare with the Temple of Artemis lying to its south. At its west end it had an atrium of which the like is rarely to be seen. The square-shaped atrium was surrounded by porticoes on three sides and the outer side was covered with parapets and turned into a promenade. The inner side of the wall built at the west end by removing the slope of the hill was designed to form a cistern. The cistern is at present repaired. To the east of the atrium was an exonarthex built at a later period and after that the narthex covered with five little cupolas. From the narthex three doors provided entrance to the main part of the church. These doors were the beginnings of three naves. According to an old tradition the middle nave was built larger that the others. After the naves and before reaching the apse transepts were built on the sides. The naves were covered with six large domes. The tomb of the saint lay in the tomb chamber underneath the middle dome. The top of the tomb was raised from the ground and was covered with mosaics. These mosaics were taken away one by one by the devoted and new ones made according to the excavation drawings were put in their place. The entrance of the tomb chamber was by means

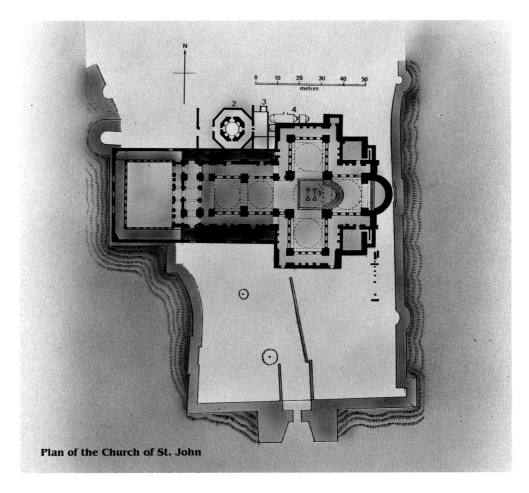

Plan of the Church of St. John

of a narrow staircase on the side of the apse. The belief that a healing powder came out of a little hole near this brought many pilgrims here to smell it in the Middle Ages. The tomb chamber was surrounded by an architrave with coloured columns and inscriptions. The raised walk in the shape of a wall led to the ambo of which only traces remain today. In 1967 the pope prayed in this church.

To the north of the edifice the building covered with a roof is a chapel constructed in the 10th century. In the apse of the chapel are frescoes of Christ in the middle with two saints on either side. Of these the one on the right is St. John. The polygonal and two-storeyed building right near the chapel was a domed treasury building. In the niches visible in the walls were kept the sacred objects of the church. The mosaics and the small altar standing on them which can be seen after these niches were built in the 12th century by the crusaders. When the mosaics were removed for repair fragments of gilded capitals were found underneath. The hexagonal baptistry of the church stands next to this. Between the baptistry and the north nave there is a fountain of fine workmanship.

A part of the church was excavated in 1920-21 and the other part was excavated later. The two tiers of columns

The Pursuit Gate (6th century AD)

93

in the north nave were erected during the first period of work. On the columns of the first floor there are the monograms of the Emperor Justinian and his wife Theodora. The edifice is being restored at present by the Museum of Ephesus. Part of the restoration expenditures are met by the Quadman family from the U.S.A.

The area on which the church stood took on the aspect of a fortress as its walls were strengthened and fortified with frequent towers against Arab attacks in the 7th and 8th centuries. The fortress had three gates. Of these the one on the west was excavated and restored whereas the excavation of the one on the east has not yet been undertaken. The gate on the south was called the Pursuit Gate. This gate was guarded by two tall towers. In the inner side there was a narrow courtyard. If the gate broke under the attacks the enemy would be destroyed in this courtyard by firing and shooting from the walls.

The walls encircling the church extend as far as the fortress on the

The Church of St. John, the Burial Area

hill. At its east end the site of the earliest settlement in Ephesus was discovered. The fortress was built in the 5th century and was used until the 12th century with various repairs. It had two gates, one on the east and the other on the west. The interior has not been excavated yet. There are cisterns. a chapel and a small mosque in it.

The Church of St. John, the western walls

THE TEMPLE OF ARTEMIS

The temple stands on the area called the English cavity to the right of the Selcuk- Kuşadası road. The place is called the English cavity because the English engineer Wood carried out the first excavations here in 1867. Almost nothing but a column is extant today of the Temple of Artemis which even in its own era was considered to be one of the seven wonders of the world. However, the excavation is still going on and the various stages of the temple are being looked into. The artifacts on display in the Artemiseum Hall of the Museum of Ephesus were discovered during recent excavations of the temple. The artifacts found in the excavations carried out by Wood were taken to the British Museum.

Strabo mentions that the Temple of Artemis was destroyed and then reconstructed seven times and that people from all over the world came to see it. In the excavations that have been going on for more than a hundred years only four stages of the temple were encountered. Small findings belonging to the earliest period were dated back to the 7th century BC. According to these findings we can say for the time being that the earliest date of the temple was that century. The 7th century BC findings were fragments of pots with geometri-

The Artemiseum

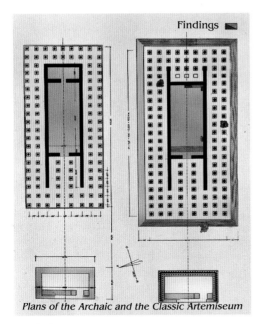

Findings ◤

Plans of the Archaic and the Classic Artemiseum

of the water in the foundaitons of the temple Theodorus filled them with coal and covered them with leather. After much labour and expenditure a large temple of a length of 115 metres and a width of 55 metres was erected. This edifice which we call the Archaic Temple was the biggest temple made of marble up to that day. The two rows of 19 metre high columns surrounding it created a forest-like aspect around it. From

cal decorations, and small ornamental objects made of gold, silver and ivory. All these objects were gifts brought to the temple from all over the world. To give presents to the temple and to ask certain things from the goddess were one of the most widespread traditions. The present the most esteemed was bulls in great numbers, for example, a hundred of them. Because of this the temple became the richest place of the province of Asia and also did business like a bank. The 7th century BC findings are supposed to have been dispersed and become mixed in with the earth from the temple which was burned and destroyed under the invasion of the Cymmerians.

In the first quarter of the 6th century BC Chersiphon of Cnossus, a renowned architect of the day, and his son Metagenes were invited to Ephesus to construct a new temple of Artemis. The site selected for the temple was that of the previous one. As the place was marshland an architect by the name of Theodorus who was familiar with the subject and who had had previous experience in Samos was also called in. To avoid the rising

The Artemiseum

among the 1st century authors, Pliny recorded that there were a total of 127 columns in the temple. Pliny also wrote that the 36 columns of the front façade were decorated with reliefs. What Pliny who had lived in the 1st century AD saw was certainly the Hellenistic temple. However, the Hellenistic temple very closely resembled the previous one. Besides, it must be noted that Pliny knew also what had been written before him. In archaeology pieces of columns with reliefs are called Columna Caelata. At first these were said to have been directly under the capitals but were later understood to have been on the bases. These pieces with reliefs were presented to Artemis by the famous King Croesus of Lydia. It is known that Croesus came to Ephesus during the construction of the temple. One of these columns with reliefs was found in the first excavations and was taken to the British Museum. On this piece there was also the inscription reading "This was presented by Croesus." The altar in front of the temple was also rebuilt as it was completely destroyed by Cymmerian attacks. A great part of the materials found in the excavations were from around the altar. Among these findings were also electrum coins known as the earliest money of the world.

In 356 BC the Archaic Temple was burned by a lunatic by the name of Hrostratos who wanted to immortalize his name. The 1st century authors could not explain how it happened that the temple which was built entirely of white marble came to burn. According to rumour the goddess could not prevent her temple from burning because the night of the fire she had gone to assist the birth of Alexander the Great. The fire caused

The Temple of Artemis, reconstruction

a psychological fright in Ephesus, it was feared that the goddess, becoming angry with them, would harm the city and without much delay the construction of a new temple was undertaken. And while this temple was under construction Alexander came to Ephesus and was greeted as a great saviour against the Persians. Alexander visited the Temple under construction and made known to the Ephesians that he was ready to meet all the expenditures of the temple up to that point in time and from that point on. The proud Ephesians would not accept an outsider to build the temple and they politely refused him by saying that it would not be appropriate for one god to build a temple for another. The Hellenistic temple stood on a podium reached by thirteen steps and was 105 metres long and 55 metres wide. The former plan and form were maintained as they were.

In the 5th century BC the first statue contest in history was held for the Temple of Artemis of Ephesus among Phidias, Polykleitos, Kresilas and Pharadmon, the famous sculptors of the day. The statue was to be that of an Amazon. When the artists finished their work the Ephesians elected as jury the same sculptors. Each sculptor evaluated his own work as first and that of Polykleitos as second. Thus the work of this sculptor deserved to be placed in the temple. The Roman copies of these statues are on display in many muesuums of Europe and of Turkey. As to which statue was by Polykleitos is a point of debate.

The Temple of Artemis was destroyed for the last time in 265 AD by the attacks of the Goths. Although the temple was rebuilt in this period in which Christianity had begun to spread it did not last long either. When it was destroyed later a large part of the construction materials

Artemis the Beautiful, detail

were used in the building of the Church of St. John and another part in the building of the Church of St.Sophia in Constantinople. This building was the temple the most destroyed by humans. The main reason for this was that the early Christians had been tortured because of Artemis.

THE CAVE OF THE SEVEN SLEEPERS

This cave is located to the east of Mount Pion. It is one of the places in Ephesus most sacred to the world of Chistianity. The place called the cave is in fact an old quarry. This side of Mount Pion was used for centuries as a quarry to provide stones for the buildings in Ephesus, thus giving rise there to many unnatural caves. The Cave of the Seven Sleepers is also one of these. In the 250s AD under the reign of the Emperor Decius seven Christian youths fled the city to avoid persecution and took refuge in one such cave. The youths who fell asleep a while later went on sleeping for two hundred years (three hundred and nine years for Moslems). When they awoke, without knowing what had gone on, they sent one of them to the city to buy bread and it became understood that they had slept for two hundred years. By that time Christianity had been the official religion. The Emperor Theodosius learning about the situation considered this to be an example of reincarnation. When the youths died they were buried in the same cave and a church was built on that place. The remains of the church are erect today. In the hope of reincarnation many of the early Christians wished to be buried there. Graves seen all around the church are related to this.

The church and the graves were brought to light in the excavations carried out in 1927.

Sarcophagus from the Cave of the Seven Sleepers

The Cave of the Seven Sleepers

THE ISA BEY BATHS

The baths are one of the earliest examples of the Turkish period existing today in the district of Selçuk. An inscription on display in the Museum of Ephesus is believed to have belonged to these baths. According to this inscription the baths were built in 1364 by the architect Hoca Ali upon the orders of Isa Bey. It is significant that this social establishment was built before the mosque, the religious establishment. This must have been caused by the principle of cleanliness, a fundamental condition of Islam. The baths lie between the Church of St. John and the Temple of Artemis. Following the street forking right from the beginning of the Selçuk-Kuşadası road for 200 metres one reaches the baths. About 50-60 metres further ahead of them lies the Mosque of Isa Bey. For years neglected, from 1983 onwards the Museum of Ephesus has been carry-ing out excavation and restoration there. The baths are a modified implementation of the Roman and Byzantine baths of the previous periods adapted to Turkish curtoms and traditions. It consists of three main divisions: the cold, the temperate and the hot. The building lies on a north-south axis and reveals a perspective which shows the cupolas lowering in the same direction. The division on the north which has two columns and is open to the sky is the cold section (dressing room) of the baths. On the sides of the walls of this section there were raised platforms with two tiers of wooden dressing rooms on them. There was a pool in the middle as understood by the traces on the floor. An intermediate space at the south-west corner of this section leads to the temperate division. This division is covered by quite a high dome which has lanterns for lighting. The floor is paved with marble. On the sides of the walls are raised platforms for resting. A door facing the entrance

The Turkish Baths (14th century AD)

leads to a small room which is also covered by a dome. This is the room where persons who could not stand much heat or who had religious purposes took their bath. The door on the south leads from the temperate division to the hot one. This is the principal bathing place of the baths. It is a good example reflecting the best architectural characteristics of the period. It has four aiwans with rectangular cells (bathing cells). As understood from the remains there was a marble bench in the middle on which the bathers perspired and were rubbed and massaged. It was covered by a big dome in the middle and smaller ones at the corners. A great part of the domes are partly destroyed. As in baths belonging to previous periods, these baths were also heated by the Hypocaust system. Tiles laid at a variety of intervals below the floor were covered by large pavings and flues of baked clay were installed in the walls. The heat and smoke of the fire burning in the furnace would circulate through this structure of the floor and through the flues in the walls before going out. The baths were thus heated. The most southern division is the furnace. In the upper part of the furnace there is a distribution network for hot and cold water. The fire burning in the furnace heated the water above. The part above the fire was made of copper. This fire circulated below the hot and temperate divisions of the bath and let out its smoke through the openings in the walls. We can see this kind of baths being used everywhere in Turkey. There are many traditions and maxims related to baths in Turkey. The most interesting of these were the bridal baths. The mother of the young man to marry selected her daughter-in-law in the baths. The girl to be a bride, dressed in her best, went to the baths with her girl friends and there they had gaieties. Examples of sayings related to baths are "women's bath" meaning a very noisy place, and "he who goes to bath perspires" meaning effort made for the realization of an important affair.

The Turkish Baths (14th century AD)

THE MOSQUE OF ISA BEY

This mosque was built on the western skirts of the Ayasuluk Hill on which stand the fortress and the Church of St. John. For topographic reasons its most ostentatious and magnificent face is the west one. It is an interesting point that it was built between the Temple of Artemis and the Church of St. John which belong to previous periods. It almost gives the impression that the temples of three different periods are in competition here. The building measures 51 by 57 metres. There is a row of shops with supporting arches at the lower level of the wall in the west façade. The main entrance on the west is reached by two separate flights of stairs of fifteen steps each mounting from either side. The mosque was built in 1375 by Aydınoğlu Isa Bey. The architect was Dımışıklı Ali from Damascus. We learn this from the inscription over the west portal. The entire west façade is covered with marble. The other faces of the edifice were built in squared blocks of stone. The west portal is framed with edgings in relief and has a protruding pointed arch which is very ostentatious. The windows in this façade are arranged in two rows one above the other. Their dimensions and decorations are different from one another. We can see here the finest examples of the stone workmanship of the period. In the lower row of windows coloured keystones were used and the upper parts of the windows on the left are decorated with stalactitic lines and holy writings. The other faces of the building are without any decoration. On the east is a portal symmetrical with that of the west. This is also called the portal of the sultan. The minaret is destroyed. The entrance on the north façade was in later periods blocked by a stone wall.

Entering the courtyard by the decorative main gate on the west covered by

The Mosque of Isa Bey (1375 AD)

The Mosque of Isa Bey, detail of portal

a diagonal vault porticoes encircling the courtyard on three sides and a fountain in the middle meet the eye. We see from the traces on the walls and the rows of columns that the portico was in two tiers. The minaret above the west entrance stands on an octagonal base, is decorated with tiles, and rises up to the external gallery. The top part was knocked down. The actual place of worship of the mosque lies to the south. This section is entered from the courtyard by a door with three pointed arches set on two columns. In the middle there are two domes set on a pointed arch rising on four large granite columns of nearly one meter diameter. The sides of the domes are covered by two rows of wooden gable roofs. Although the domes were decorated with tiles most of them have disappeared. Of the capitals on the columns three are stalactitic, thus reflecting a characteristic of the period, and one is from the Roman period in composite style. The marble niche for the imam in the south wall is new. It is a copy of the original and was built in 1989. The original niche is in the Kestane Pazarı Mosque (the Mosque of the Chestnut Market) in İzmir. It was taken there in the Ottoman period.

This mosque occupies an important place in the history of art because it was there that a second hall for the worshippers was built for the first time and also because it constituted a transitional architecture between the Seljuk and Ottoman periods.

The Mosque of Isa Bey

THE MONUMENTAL TOMB (KÜMBET)

The structure lies in a little park about 50 metres to the east of the intersection of the İzmir, Aydın and Kuşadası roads. An example of the last monumental tombs found in the district of Selçuk (Ephesus),it belongs to the end of the 14th and the beginning of the 15th centuries, hence to the period of the Principality of Aydınoğulları. It is not known to whom it belonged. The structure was built on an octagonal plan and displays careful workmanship of stone and bricks. The entrance protrudes from the building and is ornamented with nine rows of decorations. At either side of the entrance are niches with pointed arches and three rows of ornaments. Above the eaves encircling the top level of the building rises a pyramidal roof of a star plan

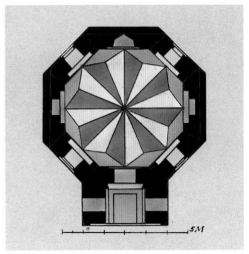

Plan of the Monumental Tomb. (Kümbet)

and twelve wedges. At first sight it reminds one of a Turkoman tent. Inside, facing the entrance stands an imam's niche with five rows of ornaments. Below the floor is the tomb chamber (Crypt).

The Monumental Tomb. (Kümbet)

THE HOUSE OF THE VIRGIN MARY

When in 1878 the book "The Life of the Virgin Mary" was publisned by Clément Brentano in French, it attracted the attention of a great number of mystics. The book contained the narrations of the paralytic nun Katerina Emmerich who was bedridden and had never in her life been in Ephesus. She began having heavenly visions in her bed which she had not left for twelve years. She recited in detail the remains of the house of the Virgin Mary and the surrounding area. In 1891 a research team headed by a priest called Yung came to the area. The research team was skeptical about the narration of the nun and wanted to prove that it was baseless.

With this thought in mind, they strolled for days in the mountains around Ephesus. In the end they decided that the place called "Panaya Kapulu" by the local people was the place narrated by the nun Katerina Emmerich. They then believed the story and changed their mind as this place fitted exactly the description. On the other hand, those who organized the research learned that the Christian Turks living in the surrounding area gathered here on the 15th of August every year to celebrate in large crowds the anniversary of the death of the Virgin Mary and that this tradition went back to very early times. The place was the ruined structure standing on the hill of Solmissos (Aladağ) in the region of Ortygia (the place where Artemis was born). Research on the building by scien-

The House of the Virgin Mary

tists brought out that the walls had the character of the 6th and 7th centuries and that the burned ashes and other things in the hearth inside the building were from the 1st century. When the building was first found, only the foundations were there. It was restored afterwards and brought to its present state (1950). The old wall remains and the walls built later were indicated by a line of red paint. The building is a small domed structure with a cross-shaped plan. It has the aspect of a small church. It is entered by the door standing between two door-like niches. This place is covered by a vault. A step leads from here to the big hall. Facing the entrance is the apse. The statue of the Virgin Mary standing in the apse is from the beginning of the century. The part of the floor with the grey paving about two metres from the apse is where the hearth was. The small room to the right of the hall is thought to be the bedroom of the Virgin Mary. In the present day, to enable the circulation of visitors a door was built in this room to lead outside. As the House of the Virgin

The statue of the Virgin Mary

Mary is highly esteemed by the Moslems too, they also worship and pray here.

The director of the French College of İzmir who had not believed the narrations of the nun at the beginning of the century changed his mind after seeing the place and replacing his actual name of Eugene Poulin by the pseudonym of Gobrielovich spent the rest of his life until his death in 1928 to propagating the authenticity of this place. On December 31st, 1892 Sister Marie de Mandat Grancey, the directress of the French Hospital of İzmir, bought in great generosity the rights of use of the house and the 100 hectares of land surrounding it and gave them to Monseigneur Timoni, the archbishop of İzmir. After this date, the importance of the place increased gradually. After the restoration of the

The interior of the House of the Virgin Mary

The interior of the House of the Virgin Mary

building such establishments as a post-office, restaurants and WCs were built to meet the needs.

Following for 7 kilometres the road forking to the right at the 2nd kilometre of the Selçuk-Aydın highway, we reach the House of the virgin Mary. Situated on the seaward slopes of Aladağ to the southwest of Mount Coressus, this place is covered by woods and has a beautiful view. Besides the House of the virgin Mary there is here a round cistern dated back to the late Roman period of which the water seems to be coming from a great number of places. As understood from the remains of foundations in the ground this cistern was once in a closed space. The wall on the slope is built as a pseudo-arch.

Before being crucified on Golgotha in Jerusalem by the opposing religious groups, Jesus, the prophet of the new religion, entrusted his mother the Virgin Mary to St. John the Apostle.

When St. john's brother Jacob was beheaded St. John and the Virgin Mary saw that they could not stay in Jerusalem and they moved on to Anatolia (41-42 AD). The Virgin Mary was 64 years old at that time. There must have been two purposes for their coming to Anatolia: firstly, to move away from danger, and secondly, to profit from the tolerance of Ephesus where people of various religions lived. Ephesus was an important missionary centre, and as a commercial centre it had both a big population and was full of people coming from and going to a variety of places. At the same time Artemis of Ephesus maintained her greatness. They must have worked quite well during the time they stayed in Ephesus because later in time Ephesus became an important centre where one of the seven churches stood.(see the Church of the Virgin Mary)

When in 1961 Pope John XXIII made known that ceremonies could be performed in the House of the Virgin Mary discussions about the place were subdued and the number of visitors gradually increased. The house was declared a place of pilgrimage. In 1967 Pope Paul VI and in 1979 Pope John-Paul II visited the House of the Virgin Mary and conducted ceremonies there which events show their esteem for the place.

The interior of the House of the Virgin Mary

The water near the House of the Virgin Mary

THE MUSEUM OF EPHESUS

THE HALL OF HOUSE OBJECTS

The Museum of Ephesus is in the district of Selçuk. Artifacts found in the excavations in Ephesus are displayed in a contemporary style in the halls of the museum according to the places where they were discovered. The first hall contains the findings relating to houses. Here are displayed artifacts found in the excavations carried out in the houses in Ephesus for nearly thirty years. Although the duration of the excavations was long the number of houses excavated was small. These were the houses standing on the slopes facing the Curetes Street. The houses on the east were first excavated and the materials like frescoes and mosaics found there were taken from their places and brought to the museum. Later it was understood that this system was not right and from then on the houses were put under protection as they were.

Portable small objects found both in the earlier and later excavations are displayed in this hall of the museum called the Hall of House Objects. Copies of a part of the artifacts were put in their original places. In the first showcase on the right small bronze artifacts found in the houses are on display. The first artifact is a cruet known by the name of Oinoche which actually was a wine holder. From the figures at both ends of its handles the cruet was dated back to the 5th century BC. Next to this are displayed a sitting Zeus of small dimensions, an Isis and small artifacts used for daily needs. These artifacts were for the most part made in the 1st, 2nd and

Asclepius (2nd century AD)

Table support with Attis (2nd century AD)

3rd centuries BC, the brightest period of Ephesus. The headless marble statue standing next to this showcase is the god of healing, Asclepius. A snake curving around a stick which was his symbol was broken. The statues of the Emperor Tiberius and his mother Livia standing in the next wall showcase are among the rare artifacts found intact and in good condition in Ephesus. As both these statues are part of the exhibition sent around the world into different countries with a view to making Anatolian civilization known, they are at present not displayed here. The bronze statue of a snake standing between the two reflects the tradition of keeping pet snakes in houses. In the Ancient period, this species of snakes which were not poisonous were regarded as the protectors of the house and the

Oinoche (wine holder), bronze (5th century BC)

destruction of them was strongly opposed. In fact pet snakes were useful animals in that they ate the small and harmful animals like mice in the house.

After these, the artifacts displayed in showcases near the middle of the hall are a part of those used for daily needs. The glass bracelets in this showcase were for children. As glass

Statuette of an Egyptian priest, bronze (6 th century BC)

Statuette of Eros on a dolphin, bronze (2nd century AD)

Head of Socrates, marble (1st century AD)

ivory objects and marble busts and portraits.

The most important artifact in the second showcase is a yellow marble head of Ganymede, the wine giver for the god Zeus.

Among the objects in the same row the bust is one of the rare busts of Menander, the comedy writer. The head next to it belongs to Socrates. It was found with the nose and a part of the face broken and missing and was

Head of Eros, marble (2nd century AD)

was cheap the bracelets were made for children, whereas for adults valuable metals were preferred. Other artifacts in the showcase are small

Priapus (2nd century AD)

later restored in conformity with the type of the Satyr Silenus which Plato mentioned in his dialogues. One of the beautiful artifacts found in the houses on the slopes of Ephesus is the Eros with a rabbit. This small size artifact represents a boy of the type of Eros trying to prevent his dog from getting at the rabbit he holds by the legs. Only a small part of the rabbit and nothing but the feet of the dog have remained.

The frescoes in the corner are of the

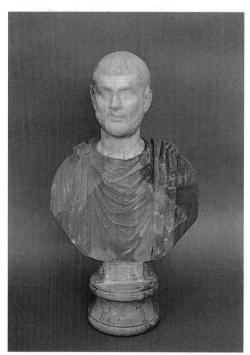

Bust of an emperor, onyx and marble (2 nd century AD)

Children's playthings, terra cotta

because of this relation. In the show-cases on the left side of the hall small objects are displayed. Among these the dark blue plate is from İznik. Furthermore, the statue of Artemis the huntress holding her bow stretched is among the beautiful statues of the museum. Following the fashion of the day this piece was executed in an archaic style.

artifacts found in the early excavations in Ephesus and transported here as they were. The statue in the niche is Artemis as huntress, and the fresco on the right, as understood from its inscription, is Socrates, represented draped in a peplos and sitting on a couch.

Of the two artifacts displayed in the showcases standing in the middle of the hall one is a marble head of Eros. The original of this work was the bronze statue of him holding a bow in his hand made in 330-320 BC by the famous sculptor Lysippus. The marble head of Eros we see is a copy made in the 2nd century AD.

The other object is a statue of an Egyptian priest with an inscription in hieroglyphics on its back made in the 6th century BC. Commercial relations between Egypt and Anatolia went on for years intensively. The statue of the Egyptian priest came to Ephesus

Bust of a child, marble (2nd century AD)

THE HALL OF THE FOUNTAINS

The second hall of the museum is the Hall of the Fountains in which the artifacts found in the monumental fountains (Nympheum) in Ephesus are displayed.

The first piece on the left is a head of Zeus dated back to the 1st century BC. The torso of aphrodite next to it, although lacking most parts, is one of the best proportioned Aphrodites in the museums of the world. The pieces displayed in the semicircular niche at the left corner are related to the statues of the Polyphemus Group as also mentioned in the chapter on the State Agora in this book. Odysseus, the hero of the epic the

Head of Zeus, marble (1st century AD)

Aphrodite, marble (1st century AD)

Odyssey by the famous author Homer, lived through a series of adventures lasting for many years on his way home after the Trojan war. One of these took place on the island on which Polyphemus, a notorious Cyclops, lived. When Odysseus and his companions from the ship came to Polyphemus' island, he caught them all and imprisoned them in a cave and he devoured several of the sailors. Then Odysseus offered the wine he had found to the Cyclops. The companions of Odysseus, using a plank the end of which was sharpened into a point, blinded the eye of the Cyclops who had become drunk after drinking the wine. Thus they escaped from the cave. The group of statues is displayed in succession. These pieces which formerly decorated the pediment of the Temple of Isis located in the middle of the State Agora of Ephesus were taken from there when the temple was destroyed later and placed on the edge of the pool of the fountain of Pollio on the

The Polyphemus Group (1st century BC)

east side of Domitian Square. The original position of the statues at the pediment of the temple are to be seen in the garden of the museum.

On the wall facing the statues of the Polyphemus Group are displayed the statues of the fountain built for the Emperor Trajan. The naked man with the bowed head is Dionysus, the god of wine. Next to it in a half-lying position is a satyr. The statues following these belong to the imperial family. The original places of the statues were drawn on the panel on the wall. The statue standing next to the panel is Androclus, the legendary founder of Ephesus. Next to it the statue with

The Resting Warrior (1st century AD)

116

Androclus and dog (1st century AD)

Aphrodite (1st century AD)

Ideal head of woman (2nd century AD)

the shell at its waist, as seen also from its style, is Aphrodite. At the left hand corner of the hall are displayed portraits and idealized heads, and at the right hand side pieces of sculpture from the Fountain of G. Laecanius Bassus situated to the east of the Temple of Domitian. This fountain is not restored yet. The most beautiful pieces of the fountain are two statues of nymphs resembling naked Aphrodites. These were modeled as if dressed in wet clothes. The dedicatory inscription of the fountain is also in this hall.

THE HALL OF RECENT DİSCOVERIES

From the Hall of the Fountains one passes to the Hall of Recent Discoveries. In the room at the west end of this hall are displayed the coins found in Ephesus. These are displayed in chronological order and the ones with bees on them are Ephesian coins. Enlargements of two of these are hung on the wall and the minting of an Ephesian coin is described on the panel nearby.

On the wall to the left of the door are shown tragic masks found in the Theatre. Where the masks were displayed in the theatre is shown on the panel. In the Roman theatre the players were all men and they used masks when necessary. Therefore the players are shown with masks in their hands in the drawing. After the masks there is a display of Ephesian lamps. All through ancient times the Ephesians had exported lamps to all the Mediterranean countries so that the Ephesian lamp was well-known. The manufacture of a lamp is shown in the display.

The bust standing in the niche of the narrow wall on the street side is of

Bust of Emperor Marcus Aurelius, marble (3rd century AD)

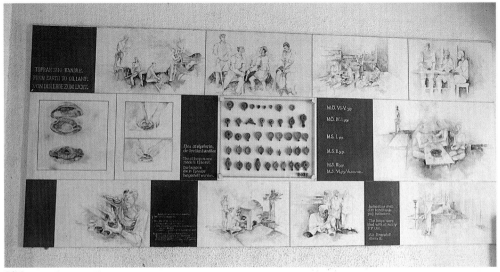

Oil lamps, terra cotta

the Emperor Marcus Aurelius. The bust of the emperor was found in recent exavations put away to keep it from harm during the reparation of a house. Therefore it was very well preserved. There are many copies of the bust in the museums around the world. The ivory frieze on display in the long showcase in the same row is unique among museums. This frieze was found burned and broken in the houses on the slopes and was restored by years of labour. Its subject is related to the wars the Emperor Trajan fought against the Parthians. The bearded men are the Parthians and the others are the Romans. The figure standing out in front is the Emperor Trajan.

The artifact displayed in the little showcase on the other side of the hall is a reliquary in the form of a small tomb. It was found in an excavation at the west end of the harbour of Ephesus and was dated back to the 9th century AD. In the showcase next to this are exhibited wine holders and the hardened wine found in Ephesus in a vessel.The wine holders were dated back from the 6th century BC to the end of the Hellenistic period.

The marble font for baptismal service standing in the middle was dated back to the 11th century. The Eros with a dolphin standing next to this was used as a tap for the pool of a house. The Eros holding a mask in his hand near it was found at the edge of the pool of another house.

Mask used in tragedy (2nd century AD)

In the last showcase in this row it is shown how the decorations of flower bouquets on a wine holder termed a Skyphos were made by reproducing by means of moulds. The positive mould is original and a rare artifact.

Ivory Frieze (2nd century AD)

THE GARDEN

On the right, the artifact in the shape of a rather big triangular plate is a fragment of an ambo. It was found in the excavations of the Church of St. John. On it there is a scene showing the Prophet Abraham sacrificing his son Ishmael. Abraham has a knife in his hand and Ishmael has a band over his eyes. The hand of God reaches out from the corner to stop the sacrifice.

The statues of Eros on a dolphin of the pool in the middle are original pieces and were used for the same purpose in unidentified pools in Ephesus. Both works were dated back to the 1st century AD from their work-manship. On the south side of the garden examples of hundreds of capitals found in Ephesus are displayed in chronological order. The first capitals are in the Ionic order and were dated back to the 6th century BC. They

Plate of parapet (6th century AD)

Pediment of the Temple of Isis, the Polyphemus Group (1st century BC)

The Sundial (3rd century AD)

were found in the excavations of the Temple of Artemis. The one with the bull's head belongs to the Basilica adjacent to the State Agora. On the pediment above the area where the capitals are exhibited there is a representation of the statues of the Polyphemus Group as they stood in their original place, the pediment of the Temple of Isis. The darker statues are the ones displayed in the Hall of Fountains of the museum and the white ones are the fragments that could not be found in the excavations. Stelae of offering and tombs standing at the west wall of the garden date from the Hellenistic to the end of the Roman period. Of the figures on the stelae those shown lying or naked represent the deceased, the ones near them the relatives, and the smaller ones the slaves. The intact sarcophagus in front of these is known as the Sarcophagus with the

Muses because of the reliefs of Muses around it. It was found accidentally in the necropolis outside the walls of Ephesus. Excavations in the necropolis are not yet begun in Ephesus. The sarcophagus was used twice as understood from its inscription.

The lion-headed griffins exhibited in the middle are a part of the decorations of the Monumental Tomb of Belevi. In the village of Belevi which can be reached by a road forking out after 15 kilometres from Ephesus on the way to İzmir, there is a tumulus and a monumental tomb with a pyramidal roof like the mausoleum in Halicarnassus. A sarcophagus of fine workmanship found in the monument for which there was no knowledge as to whom it belonged is also on display here. The many-lined inscription

Relief of helmet (2nd century BC)

Capital with a bull's head

behind the sarcophagus was originally in the harbour of Ephesus and in the Byzantine period it was taken from there and used as part of an ambo in the Church of St. John. The inscription is a very important document concerning the harbour laws. It is therefore also known as the Monument of Ephesus.

THE HALL OF TOMB OBJECTS

A part of the artifacts found in the tombs around Ephesus are on display in this hall. On the panel to the right of the entrance of the hall are shown examples of the tombs in Anatolia. In the showcase on the left are displayed pots from the Mycenaean tomb found accidentally during the arrangement of a car park for the Church of St. John. These artifacts dated back to the 13th and 14th centuries BC are the earliest pieces in the museum. The larger bowl was probably a wine holder and is decorated with figures of octopi. In the showcase next to this, small tomb gifts dated back from the 6th century BC to the 1st century AD are on display. The marble tomb stele in the same row was dated back to the Hellenistic period. The sarcophagus of baked clay in the showcase is of the Clazomenae type. Uncovered in the excavations of the Mercantile Agora of Ephesus, it is one of the rare archaic artifacts in the city. The sarcophagi called the Clazomenae type were given this name because they were first found in the city of the same name situated 60 kilometres to the west of Ephesus. In the sarcophagus there were also messages as gifts. At the time of the burial, the relatives of the deceased would leave presents in the tomb according to their budgets. To put a coin between the lips of the deceased was also an important tradition.

At the corner to the right of the Clazomenae sarcophagus are displayed the findings from the Cave of the Seven Sleepers of Ephesus and on the panel are pictures of the cave. One of these is an enlargement of a 16th century engraving kept at present in the Museum of Turkish and Islamic Art in Istanbul. The engraving shows seven persons in Islamic

The sarcophagus with Muses (3rd century AD)

Burial types in Anatolia

Hellenistic period. The bracelets were in general used as objects of ornament for children.

The large tomb stele on display at the next corner, according to the inscription on it, belonged to Olympia, daughter of Diocles. The bust of Olympia in the stele which is of a very rare shape has a sad expression. The head, draped in a shawl, must have carried a golden diadem as understood from the hole on it. To keep the diadem from being stolen the upper half of the stele was closed by an iron frame. The top of the piece has the aspect of a Doric temple.

clothes sleeping in the cave and their dog Kıtmir. According to the Mohammedan belief the sleepers of the cave have slept for three hundred and nine years. The other engraving is taken from the Calendar of Saints of Basileus II. In this one the seven young men sleeping in the same cave are shown in 9th century Christian clothing. According to Christian myths the youths who took refuge in the cave slept for two hundred years. For centuries the Cave of the Seven Sleepers was chosen as a place of burial by the Christians who wanted to be reincarnated and tombs were built almost everywhere around the church standing in the cave. The artifacts displayed at the corner are urns and osteothecas. One of these, of onyx much used in the area for touristic purposes, is in the shape of an amphora.

In the showcase for glassware are displayed the glass objects found in the excavations in Ephesus. These were used as jars to hold wine, medicines and perfume. The coloured ones are glass vessels of Phoenician type which people loved to use in the

In the showcase at the last corner on the left there is again a display of tomb gifts found around Ephesus. Next to it the history and reliefs of the Mother Goddess Cybele, the most ancient goddess of Anatolia, are on display. The relief showing Cybele sitting in a niche, made in the 5th century, is of a well-known type. The others are bas-reliefs. Cybele is shown in the middle with Zeus on one side of her and Attis, her high priest, on the other. On the panel above, the history and evolution of Cybele in Anatolia are explained by drawings and writings, and the important cult centres of the goddess are shown on the map of Turkey nearby. The earliest reliefs of the mother goddess in Turkey are those found in Çatalhöyük near Konya. They were dated back to the 7th century BC. As it can also be seen from the drawings, these statuettes showed the mother goddess fat and fecund. At the present day, they are exhibited at the Museum of Anatolian Civilizations of Ankara.

THE HALL OF ARTEMIS

Three statues of Artemis found hidden in the excavation of the Prytaneum to the north of the State Agora of Ephesus and small artifacts presented to the temple are exhibited in this hall. The first exhibit on the left is a moulage copy the original of which is in the museum of History and Archaeology of Vienna. A fragment of the altar standing in front of the Temple of Artemis, it has reliefs of Amazons on it. In the big niche near it stands the famous Artemis of Ephesus. Because of its large size it is also known as Artemis the Colossal. It stands calmly looking into the distance. She wears a long headdress decorated with reliefs of two rows of temples. The breastlike swells on her chest were first thought to be breasts, then bodies of bees (the emblem of Ephesus is a bee), but then the thesis that these were the testes of the bulls sacrificed to the goddess gained weight. Her arms are stretched forward. It is known that the earliest statues of Artemis were made of wood and that to keep them from rotting they were frequently smeared with sweet-smelling oils and covered with coloured silk cloths. Apart from the face, the hands that remained uncovered were made of ivory or gold. It is understood that this tradition was continued also in the marble statues of the goddess. The hands are missing from the wrist out. It is certain that the wrists were not broken but made on purpose in this way to fasten on hands. The goddess has a richly decorated belt round her waist and lower down there are decorations of rows of animals, such as bulls, lions and griffins symbolizing her superiority, shown in partitions. The big reliefs of lions on her arms are strong evidence that the goddess was in the stage of transition from Cybele. In all the statues of Cybele there were

Artemis the Colossal (1st century AD)

lions at her side. The statue called Artemis the Colossal was made in the 1st century AD as the continuation of an earlier type.

A smaller statue of Artemis on display on the other narrow wall of the hall is know as Artemis the Beautiful. Indeed it was quite intact when found, particularly the face was untouched. It has the same form and posture. The goddess has stretched her arms forward as seen on coins. At her feet on both sides are her most sacred animals, the deer. On both sides of her head her sacred animals stand in a halo, round her neck she has a pearl necklace and at her sides are nikes, the symbol of her victory. The zodiac under the necklace shows the goddess' power over the heavens. The traces of gilding on her neck are an indication that the statue was once completely gilded. According to its style, the statue called Artemis the Beautiful was created about fifty years after Artemis the Colossal.

The marble block standing to the left of the statue of Artemis the Beautiful is a peace treaty between Ephesus and Alexandria in Egypt. On one side of the wreath in the centre there are the reliefs of Artemis of Ephesus and on the other those of Serapis.

On the other side of the statue of Artemis stands another statue of her, a small and unfinished one. The lead

Relief showing Artemis and Serapis, marble (238-244 AD)

pipe in front of this belonged to the water duct extending to the Artemiseum. As a symbol of wealth it was made of lead with joints cut out of marble. The architectural decoration of classical design at the foot of the wall is of a fine workmanship. The horse near the same wall belonged to one of the quadrigae (chariots drawn by four horses) standing on one of the corners of the altar, a structure in the shape of an angular U, situated in front of the Temple of Artemis. The head and neck of the horse are particularly life-like. The architectural fragments to the left of the exit door belonged to the temple. The lions' heads were used as gargoyles. In the Byzantine period certain architectural elements of the temple were used in other constructions, and decorations were broken here and there. The frieze with the egg motif displayed here is one of these. The egg motif was broken and replaced by a cross.

On the upper part of the wall near the Hall of the Tomb Objects there is a drawing of the Temple of Artemis, one of the seven wonders of the world, and on the left corner a picture of the earliest excavations of the temple. In the showcase here a part of the gifts presented to the altar of the goddess are displayed. These are of valuable materials like gold and ivory as well as of bronze and marble. Glasslike small objects are of mountain crystal. It is not known for what purpose they were used.

Artemis of Ephesus (2nd century AD)

THE HALL OF THE EMPERORS

Marble objects relating to busts and temples of emperors are displayed in this hall. The statue to the right of the entrance is that of the Consul Stefanos. It was found in the Curetes Street and was dated back to the 6th century. Stefanos who was a governor of Ephesus is shown with one hand lifted and about to drop a handkerchief. He was thus starting a game in the stadium or the theatre. The portraits of heads near the entrance belong to the period of the Holy Roman Empire. The one with the thick neck and small ears was probably a wrestling emperor. On the west wall of the hall, the marble frieze of the temple of the Emperor Hadrian is displayed together with a picture. During the restoration of the temple the original was brought to the museum and a copy of the frieze was placed in the temple to avoid the decaying of the original under weather conditions. Androclus, the founder of Ephesus, the procession of Dionysus, and the Amazons are the main subjects represented on the frieze. The last section of the frieze

Bust of Julia Paula (3rd century AD)

consisting of four parts differs in style from the others. The reason for this is believed to be that the fourth block of the frieze was damaged during the rebuilding of the temple which was destroyed in the earthquakes of the mid-4th century.

Next to the frieze of the Temple of Hadrian stands the altar of the Temple of Domitian. During the excavation of the temple the altar was found in fragments and was restored in the

The Hall of the Emperors

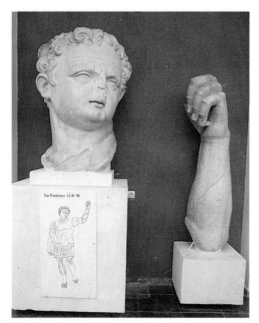

Head and arm of Emperor Domitian (81-96 AD)

statue of the emperor, believed to have stood between the temple and the altar in front of it, is supposed to have been 7 metres high together with its base.

The two statues standing to the right of the exit door are the Emperor Augustus and his wife Livia. These statues were found broken in the basilica near the upper Agora and were restored. Crosses were engraved on their foreheads when they were broken. Thus we can say that these statues were broken in the early Christian period.

museum remaining true to the original. On the narrow face of the altar there is a relief showing a sacrificial bull in front of a smaller altar, and on the larger face reliefs of weapons and armours.

A head of a statue of monumental dimensions displayed on the wall facing this altar is the Emperor Domitian. A part of the arms and legs of the statue were also found together with the head during the excavations. The

Busts of the Emperor Augustus and his wife Livia (1st century AD)

Statue of Consul Stefanos (6th century AD)

Frieze of the Temple of Hadrian (2nd century AD)

Portraits (2nd and 3rd centuries AD)

Relief on the altar of the Temple of Domitian